Colorado's HISTORIC CHURCHES

†

Linda Wommack

THE
History
PRESS

Published by The History Press
Charleston, SC
www.historypress.com

Copyright © 2019 by Linda Wommack
All rights reserved

Cover photo of American Mothers Chapel, El Paso County, Colorado, courtesy of Cindy
Kuhn Photography.

First published 2019

Manufactured in the United States

ISBN 9781467142823

Library of Congress Control Number: 2019932547

Dedicated to my grandchildren:

Brandy May
Krystal Leanne
Kayla Beth
William Ray

I thank God for their presence in my life.

Contents

Preface

The historic churches included in this work are all listed in the Colorado State Register and/or the National Register of Historic Places and are so designated by the register numbers. Particular attention has been given to the Colorado Directory of Religious Historic Properties.

With the establishment of a church in a growing community, a sense of local pride and social fellowship often developed. The church served the community not only as a house of worship but also as a place for celebration, such as weddings and baptisms. The church also served in sad times, providing a place for funerals and memorial services. Through good times and bad, the local church served the community in various ways, including fundraising for the needy and providing refuge for the destitute. Through my research into the history of these glorious buildings, I discovered many interesting tidbits associated with several of these historic churches. A few of these buildings, such as Denver's Sacred Heart Church and Grand Junction's Handy Chapel, faced destruction. Each was saved by the dedication of its congregation. Some of the structures that are featured in the preservation lists are closed to the public.

Further research into individual churches often led to colorful histories. From scandal to corruption, from bigotry to murder, nearly every house of worship in this volume has a unique story.

Here is the church
And here is the steeple
Open it up and see all the people

CHAPTER I

The South Platte River Valley

Every valley shall be filled in, every hill made low. The crooked roads
straightened, the rough ways smoothed.
—Luke 3:5

The Native Americans—including the Arapahos, Cheyennes and
Sioux—had been using the South Platte River Road long before
gold was discovered at the confluence of Cherry Creek and the
South Platte River in 1858. Following the discovery, as thousands used the
road traveling west for the gold fields, others settled in the valley and built
homes and communities.

Due to the arrival of the Union Pacific Railroad, Logan County was
created in 1887 from portions of Weld County. The South Platte River
runs through a portion of Sterling, the Logan County seat. Sterling's first
Catholic church was erected one year later.

A Catholic missionary, William J. Howlett, is credited with building the
church. Howlett later wrote, "From the graders [railroad] on the road I
collected enough money to buy a block ground in Sterling, and in 1888 I
built a frame church, which was dedicated by Bishop Nicholas C. Matz, June
24, 1888, the feast of its patron, St. John the Baptist."[1]

Severe weather, common on Colorado's eastern plains, damaged the
building more than once. On the third occasion, large hail demolished the
church. As the Catholic parishioners languished with no house of worship,
they asked for Bishop Matz to assign a resident priest. In 1908, Father Peter

U. Sasse came to Sterling. In time, with help from the congregation, Father Sasse was able to purchase a lot on South Third Street.

In 1911, with approval from the archdiocese, Father Sasse hired the Black Hills Company, an architectural firm in Deadwood, South Dakota, to construct the St. Anthony's Roman Catholic Church. The Romanesque Revival building was built of local pressed brick atop a foundation of natural stone. The deep-red brick walls were enhanced with sand-colored trim. The entrance featured an arched frame, above which was a large round window with leaded stained glass. On either side of the entrance stood tall square towers with arched windows. Frescoed walls dominated throughout the interior. Three altars were placed side by side, with the center altar including a bas relief painting of *The Last Supper*. Bishop Matz made the trip to Sterling from Denver to conduct the dedication service, held on November 5, 1911. More than five hundred Catholics attended the ceremony.

Two years later, in 1913, Father Sasse was able to hire a contractor to build a two-story rectory on the north side of the church. This was followed by a convent and a school in 1917. (National Register, 6/3/1982, 5LO.38.)

The All Saints Episcopal Church was built in 1915. Constructed of red brick, the house of worship contained several elements of the Late Gothic Revival style. The many Gothic arched stained-glass windows were a distinct feature. One hundred years later, descendants of the original congregation remain the core membership of the All Saints Episcopal Church. (National Register, 3/8/2000, 5LO.437.)

In 1919, the Presbyterians hired J.C. Fulton, a Pennsylvania architect, to design and build their new church. The First United Presbyterian Church, built on Fourth Street, was built of local pressed brick. The speckled buff-colored brick walls were detailed with limestone trim. Fulton used various forms of the Classic Revival designs while incorporating aspects of Greek and Roman as well. The most evident was the dome, which rose from the center of the roof. The entrance to the church included a two-story portico with four fluted columns. Inside, a large semicircular auditorium boasted seating for five hundred people. Golden oak was used for the pulpit and the wrapping balcony. Leaded stained glass adorned the auditorium and was also a feature in the rotunda. (National Register, 6/3/1982, 5LO.37.)

Morgan County was named for the 1860 fort erected high on a bluff overlooking the South Platte River. Both the fort and the county were named in honor of Civil War veteran Colonel Christopher A. Morgan.

In 1903, a Danish immigrant couple, Reverend Jens Madsen and his wife, Anne Marie, established the Eben Ezer Sanitarium for tubercular patients.

Bishop Nicholas C. Matz helped build Catholic churches across the prairie. *Courtesy of Denver Public Library.*

Years later, Mrs. Bertha Gade, who was a young girl at the time, recalled the event: "In 1902 Rev. Madsen, who later founded Eben Ezer, came to our church once a month. He was looking for a place to build a sanitarium for tubercular patients, and finally decided on Brush. In 1903 he moved here and was our pastor for a year."[2]

It was an elaborate facility with walkways throughout the thirty-five landscaped acres. In 1918, Reverend Madsen enlisted the architectural expertise of fellow Danish immigrants the Baerresons brothers of Denver to construct a church. Built of red brick, the walls were trimmed with rhyolite from Del Norte, Colorado. Danish Gothic elements were used throughout. The triangular roof included gables and three triangular panels along the sides, comprising piers and recessed panels, trimmed with rhyolite. Gothic arched windows contained stained glass.

Inside, the hand-polished pews glistened with colored streams of light from the windows. The pulpit, framed by the chancel wall, was built of brick and topped with local stone slabs. (National Register, 6/3/1982, 5MR.467.)

The Rankin Presbyterian Church, located at 420 Clayton Street, was built in 1907. The building is a wonderful example of Gothic Revival architecture, including a steeply pitched cross-gabled roof, pointed arch openings and a fabulous crenelated square tower. An addition was added to the south side in 1963. (National Register, 7/20/2007, 5MR.614.)

Conversely, the German Evangelical Immanuel Congregational Church exemplified the features of the Late Gothic Revival architectural style. Constructed in 1927 at 209 Everett Street, the house of worship was designed by Denver architect Walter Simon. The brick building included large triple windows in pointed arched frames and a tall square tower over the arched entrance. (National Register, 10/14/2005, 5MR.832.)

About twenty miles north of Brush was the small farming community of Antelope Springs. In 1915, Mr. and Mrs. Earl T. White donated an acre of their land to the community for a church. The two-story clapboard church featured many elements of the Carpenter Gothic style of architecture. The

The Antelope Springs church is north of Brush. *Courtesy of Charles Tribbey.*

windows were framed in the traditional Gothic arch style. The steep pitched roof held the square belfry. The extended entrance to the church featured double doors.

The Antelope Springs Church, although a rural church, included electric lighting. The electric power was provided by a battery, which was recharged as needed by a Ford Model T automobile. Over the years, the building was renovated, including the installation of a furnace.

An oft-told story involves a new minister. Not pleased with the open prairie and few trees, he made the comment that "jack rabbits out here have to find a fence post for shade." For many years, the doors of the church were never locked. (Colorado State Register, 5MR.909.)

Washington County was created from portions of Weld County in 1887. The region, with Akron as the county seat, has always been a vital rural ranch and farming area. When Akron was platted as a railroad town in 1882, the Akron Town Site and Improvement Company was formed. In a town meeting, officials told the gathered citizens, "With more American nerve and enterprise than can be found anywhere else. Akron, only ten years hence will be a city of 50,000. God has placed the elements of unlimited mineral and agricultural wealth around us."[3]

The First United Methodist Church was built on the southwest corner of Ash and Third Streets. The clapboard building, built in the Queen Anne style, included arched windows beneath the steep pitched roof. At the corner of the church, a bell tower with a dormered mansard roof rose high above the church. From the base of the bell tower, a gabled entryway welcomed the parishioners. (5.WS.92.)

Weld County, one of the original counties, was named for the first secretary of Colorado Territory, Lewis L. Weld. The South Platte River and its tributaries—including Boulder Creek, the Cache la Poudre River, Big and Little Thompson Rivers and St. Vrain Creek—helped in the creation of not only Colorado's richest agricultural county but also one of the most productive in America. The town of Greeley, named for Horace Greeley, was the center of Union Colony and became the county seat in 1870.

In 1911, the corner lot of Tenth Avenue and Tenth Street was purchased by the local Baptist congregation. Architect T. Robert Wieger was hired to build the First Baptist Church. Following the Classical Revival style, the building was constructed atop a raised foundation. Built of beige brick, the church resembled a classical temple, with Ionic double columns flanking the entrance. Inside, the large sanctuary with a beamed ceiling featured stained-glass windows. In 1927, an organ was purchased from Denver's Orpheum Theater. (National Register, 11/25/1987, 5WL.1251.)

Adams County, created in 1902, was named for Governor Alva Adams. The area, known for its rich, fertile soil, had been supplying agricultural produce to Denver markets since the Pikes Peak Gold Rush of 1858. The Denver Pacific Railroad town of Brighton, formally Hughes Station, became the county seat.

In 1886, the Presbyterian congregation of Brighton built its Presbyterian church at what would become 147 South First Avenue. The red brick building, constructed in the Gothic Revival style, became Brighton's first permanent church building. Four years later, the addition of a bell tower completed the building.

In 1975, the Presbyterian church was purchased by the Adams County Historical Society. Restored as a project of the Colorado bicentennial events in 1976, the former Presbyterian church is used for community events. (AM. 65.)

The precious commodity of gold had been discovered at the confluence of the South Platte River and Cherry Creek in 1858 by William Greenberry Russell, creating a frenzy of mass migration the likes of which the Rocky Mountain region had never seen. In the midst of this frenzy, known as the Pikes Peak Gold Rush, mining supply settlements on either side of Cherry

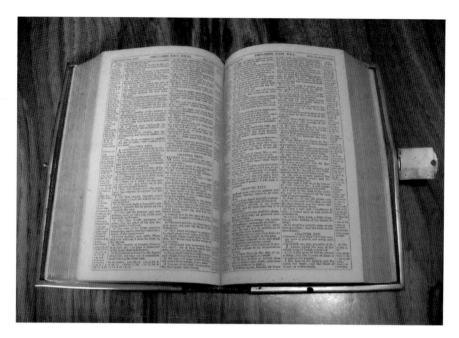

This "pocket" Bible belonged to the author's great-grandmother Olga Hoglund Berglund. *Author's collection.*

Greeley's First Baptist Church. *Courtesy of Denver Public Library.*

Creek were established. Tent cities and eventually log cabins were erected on both sides of Cherry Creek. The town of Auraria lay on the west bank, while Denver City was sited on the east side. By 1859, Denver City, named for the Kansas territorial governor James W. Denver, became the primary stopover site to the riches held by the Rocky Mountains. General William Larimer of Leavenworth, Kansas, laid out the town of Denver City with a futuristic eye. Denver, the "Queen City," as it would come to be called, would soon encompass the land east of the Platte River, nearer to Cherry Creek, with plenty of room for growth. Businesses opened, homes were built and a sense of stability slowly evolved.

On November 15, 1865, Colorado's first black congregation, Zion Baptist, was formed by a group of seventeen black settlers, a few of whom were former slaves, including Denver businessman Barney Ford. In 1867, the group built the Zion Baptist Church, a small twenty-by-forty-foot frame structure on two lots at today's Arapahoe and Twentieth Streets. When completed, the new church was one of the first black churches built west of the Mississippi River. Original founders Robert Bozier and Thomas J. Riley were the first deacons of the church, and Reverend William Norrid, also a founder, served as the congregation's first pastor.

About ten years later, under the leadership of Reverend R.M. Duling, the original frame building was replaced with a fine red brick structure. A few years later, the congregation's third pastor, Reverend William Gray, began a prison ministry, one of the first in the country.

In 1899, Reverend John E. Ford began his ten-year service as pastor of Zion Baptist Church. Incidentally, the reverend's wife, Dr. Justina L. Ford, was Denver's first black female physician. In 1911, the Zion Baptist congregation purchased the former Calvary Baptist Church building at the northwest corner of Ogden Street and Twenty-Fourth Avenue. The Zion Baptist Church has remained at this location, serving the community. In 2015, the proud members of Zion Baptist Church celebrated their 150th anniversary.[4]

Denver's oldest neighborhood, Auraria, was originally a townsite established by William Green Russell and his group of gold prospectors in 1858. By the 1870s, the area—bounded by Cherry Creek, West Colfax Avenue and the South Platte River—had evolved into a mixed residential neighborhood. In 1876, the same year Colorado achieved statehood, Episcopalian bishop John F. Spaulding built the Emmanuel Episcopal Church on Tenth Street in the Auraria neighborhood. Built of natural sandstone in the Gothic Revival style, there were also elements of the Romanesque style, such as the Gothic arched windows.

By 1903, the ethnic composition of the neighborhood had changed. It was that year that the local "Little Israel" community along West Colfax Avenue, known as the Shearith Israel congregation, purchased the church. The Jewish congregation made several changes while converting the building into a synagogue, which was renamed the Emmanuel Shearith Israel Chapel. Those changes included the placing of the Star of David atop the roof as well as a Hebrew inscription over the entrance. However, in religious respect and tolerance, the traditional Gothic elements of the edifice remained intact. In 1963, the Emmanuel Shearith Israel Chapel was sold to a private owner, who converted the building into an artist's studio. In 1976, during the Colorado bicentennial, the building received a renovation by the local firm of Gale Abels and Associates. The Emmanuel Shearith Israel Chapel, Denver's oldest standing church, was placed in the Colorado State Register of Historic Properties. (December 1, 1969, 5DV.120.)

In 1874, construction was underway for the new Grace Community Methodist Church, located in the 1300 block of Bannock Street just west of downtown Denver. During this time, Colorado's first territorial governor, John Evans, suffered a personal loss. Evans's daughter, Josephine Evans Elbert, died suddenly. Following the death of his daughter, Evans commissioned the construction of the Evans Memorial Chapel at the corner of Thirteenth and Bannock Streets. The brown rhyolite chapel, designed in the Gothic Revival style, featured the original cornerstone of

The first Zion Baptist Church was located on Denver City's only business street. *Courtesy of Denver Public Library.*

Denver's Emmanuel Shearith Israel Chapel. *Courtesy of Denver Public Library.*

the Grace Community Methodist Church. The Evans Memorial Chapel served the Methodist community until 1959.

In 1959, the many buildings of the Grace Community Methodist Church were dismantled or destroyed in the name of "progress." Fortunately, one building was saved, the Evans Memorial Chapel. The religious structure was moved to a pristine location on the campus of the University of Denver. The university is the former Colorado Seminary, founded by John Evans in 1864. Thus, it is Colorado's oldest institution of higher education. (National Register, 12/27/1974, 5DV.174.)

Following the arrival of the Denver Pacific and Kansas Pacific Railroads to the Denver area in 1870, the prospects for employment in the booming city brought a new rush of fortune seekers. Many of these new residents were the Irish railroad workers who had settled in the northeast section of Denver. With such an influx of the Irish Catholic to the area, Bishop Joseph Projectus Machebeuf saw the need for a new parish.

Bishop Machebeuf enlisted the help of the local Jesuit Order to secure funding for the new church while he searched for an affordable site. In 1879, Machebeuf paid $2,000 for five lots on the southwest corner of Larimer and Twenty-Eighth Streets. This area, located between Denver's railroad tracks and streetcar lines on Champa and Larimer Streets and Twenty-Third and Downing Streets, would become known as Five Points. Later, much of the residential section became the Curtis Park neighborhood.

Local architect Emmet Scott Anthony was hired to build Denver's first Irish Catholic church, Sacred Heart Church. While Anthony's design included the traditional cruciform style, he also added his own unique style to the building. Anthony contracted with local mason Ronald P. MacDonald to erect the brick building. To incorporate the Gothic elements of his design, the firm of McPhee and McGinnity was hired to provide the intricate woodwork. The two-story church featured tall arched windows with colored glass, framed with fine woodworking. Rather than the traditional placement of the steeple in the center or corner of the church, Anthony chose to build his steeple over the Larimer Street arched entrance. The towering steeple, graced with Gothic windows on all four sides, included a large metal bell that could be heard throughout the neighborhood.

The interior featured the decorative woodworking of McPhee and McGinnity. The ceiling of the sanctuary was enhanced with wooden arched beams, as were the end-caps of the neatly lined pews. The raised wooden platform for the altar included ornately carved woodwork, highlighted by the natural light from the skylight above.

Adjacent to the church, a small frame house was built for the pastor's home. For the first pastor of the new church, Bishop Machebeuf selected a member of the Jesuit Order, Father John Baptise Guida, a professor of philosophy, at Georgetown University. Perhaps Bishop Machebeuf chose Father Guida as a token for his appreciation for the Jesuit Order's assistance in making the new church a reality. Nevertheless, it must have been a bit disheartening for the Irish Catholics that an Irish priest was not chosen.

On September 12, 1879, the doors of Sacred Heart Church were opened to the Catholic worshipers, where Father Guida celebrated the first mass, a Mass of the Sacred Heart. By April 1880, Father Guida was offering mass three times daily. On April 25, 1880, Sacred Heart Church was finally dedicated, with Vicar General Raverdy singing the high mass. In the fall of 1880, the basement of the church was transformed into classrooms for a Catholic school.

Sacred Heart Church became a prominent church throughout the Denver area. Among the active members were Mrs. J.J. "Molly" Brown and Horace A.W. Tabor and his wife, Elizabeth "Baby Doe" Tabor. Both couples had gained their wealth from the silver mines of Leadville. Very rarely did Baby Doe Tabor ever miss a Sunday mass. Because of his Catholic wife's devotion to the church, Tabor provided the funds and labor for the erection of a wrought-iron fence along the Twenty-Eighth Street side of the church that remains to this day.[5] During the economic depression following the repeal of the Sherman Silver Purchase Act in 1893, Horace Tabor lost his fortune. By April 1899, Tabor and his wife were living in a suite at the Windsor Hotel, just a few blocks from Sacred Heart Church. On Wednesday, April 5, Tabor fell ill and was bedridden. A doctor diagnosed the sixty-nine-year-old Tabor's condition as appendicitis. Because of his age, there was nothing that could be done for Tabor. When it became apparent to all that Tabor would not live much longer, Baby Doe Tabor sent for Father Edward Barry from Sacred Heart Church. Father Barry arrived at the Windsor Hotel suite that afternoon, Sunday, April 9, 1899. There, Father Barry baptized the former "Silver King of Colorado" and performed communion and the last rites. After Father Barry had completed his tasks, Tabor replied, "This is the happiest moment of my life. I am at peace and resigned to the will of God."[6]

Horace Austin Warren Tabor died the next day. His large funeral was held at Sacred Heart Church on April 14, 1899. Father Barry officiated over the Requiem Mass. Burial followed in the Catholic section, Mount Calvary, of the City Cemetery.[7]

A few days following the funeral, Tabor's widow, Baby Doe, in a gesture of gratitude, presented Father Barry with several elaborate flower vases. These vases grace the ledges of the altar to this day. When Baby Doe Tabor died in Leadville in 1935, a funeral was held in that city. Later, a second funeral was held at Sacred Heart Church. Meanwhile, Tabor's body had been removed from the old City Cemetery and reinterred at Mount Olivet Cemetery, where Elizabeth "Baby Doe" was buried.

Sadly, over the decades, Sacred Heart Church became a victim of neglect. In 1948, Father John Casey became pastor of the church. Casey had a long history with the church and therefore was very passionate about its preservation. Casey's parents had been married in the church. Following his birth, Casey had been baptized there and later served as an altar boy. At the time Casey became pastor, the majority of the Irish parishioners had moved away, and the Curtis Park neighborhood had dramatically deteriorated. This was due in large part to changes of Larimer Street, which by this time had gained the moniker of "Skid Row."

During his tenure as pastor, Father Casey worked tirelessly to restore Sacred Heart Church to its former glory. In an effort to repair the steeple, structural engineers informed Father Casey that the wooden supports were not only rotting but were also straining under the weight of the heavy church bell. Reluctantly, Father Casey was forced to take down the steeple, replacing it with a simple wooden tower capped with a steel crown. When the skylight over the altar fell, Father Casey replaced it with a simple wooden plank in the ceiling. Then he enlisted the expertise of parishioner Carlota Espinoza, who created a mural of the resurrection of Christ on the replaced woodwork.

For the next two decades, Father Casey devoted his life to his parishioners and the church. In an interview given to the *Rocky Mountain News* in 1968, Father Casey said, "In spite of the age of the church and the neighborhood, even visitors notice the new young spirit and the friendliness of the people. I think I've spent more time with a paint brush in my hand in the last twenty years than I have with religious objects."[8]

With the help of the congregation, Father Casey was able to replace various pieces of furniture as well as the organ and confessionals. When funds became available, Father Casey purchased the empty lot next to the church. In time, with volunteer help, the lot became a park, used for outdoor church activities.

Local preservationists, in an effort to facilitate urban renewal, formed Historic Denver Inc. In 1973, the group met with Father Casey, and a conference on historic preservation was held at Sacred Heart Church. On March 8, 1975, Sacred Heart Church was the first historic property to be declared a Denver landmark by the city council.[9]

The Catholic archdiocese took over the operations of Sacred Heart Church in 1988. On July 1 of that year, Father Marcus M. Medrano became the new priest. Medrano told the press, "The oldness of the parish creates many challenges. My people and I, poor though we are, will continue the struggle to keep Sacred Heart a great parish."[10]

Father Medrano, who also was raised in the church, did indeed struggle with his mission. With help from parishioners, he was able to continue the restoration started by Father Casey. However, the parish had meager funds. At one point, Father Medrano was forced to ask the archdiocese for $5,000 to replace the broken furnace. Father Medrano later recalled, "One winter the place was so cold you could see your breath and the holy water froze."[11]

Over the ensuing years, the Colorado Historical Society has awarded grants for further restoration of the church. It has been a slow but steady process. Today, Denver's oldest continuous Catholic house of worship, Sacred Heart Church, remains a historic landmark. (5DV.997.)

In the year 1882, the first Jewish synagogue in Denver, Temple Emanuel, was built. Designed by one of Denver's leading architects, Frank E. Edbrooke, the building incorporated several elements of several

Left: Sacred Heart Church, where many of Denver's elite worshiped, including Horace and "Baby Doe" Tabor. *Courtesy of Denver Public Library.*

Below: Denver's Temple Emmanuel. *Courtesy of Denver Public Library.*

architectural styles, including Moorish and Romanesque details. Tragically, a fire in 1897 destroyed most of the building. Undaunted, the Jewish congregation rebuilt the house of worship in brick. (National Register, 10/10/1978, 5DV.144.)

St. Joseph's Roman Catholic Church was commissioned in 1888. Located in Denver's west side neighborhood, the church was built at 600 Galapago Street. The Victorian Gothic edifice, built of brick, is one of few buildings of the era that included American-made stained-glass windows with clear prisms. The Gothic elements were carried out in the interior as well. Several columns were decorated with ornamental millwork. (National Register, 6/3/1982, 5DV.25.)

In 1887, Robert S. Roeschlaub, Denver's first licensed architect, was hired to build Denver's Trinity Methodist-Episcopal Church. Although this was Roeschlaub's first building, it is considered by many architects and historians to be his finest architectural achievement.[12] Located in the heart of downtown Denver, at the corner of Eighteenth Street and Broadway, the Richardsonian style of architecture employed by Roeschlaub became his crowning jewel. Natural sandstone, a light-beige rhyolite from the Castle Rock quarries, was used throughout the construction. Large blocks of the sandstone, in varied sizes and heights, were laid in distinct places, lending a horizontal band effect to the foundation of the church. Roeschlaub blended the Richardsonian style with elements of Gothic masonry evident in the many gables and cornered towers.[13]

The many arched windows, all strategically placed in sets of three, were manufactured by Healy and Millet of Chicago, Illinois. The tall tower, at the corner of Eighteenth Street and Broadway, included the signature arched windows, as well as a belfry, capped with a handsome stone steeple. Utah sandstone, with its purple hue, was used to create three horizontal stripes integrated with the Castle Rock rhyolite in the steeple. When completed in 1888, due to the central location, the steeple could be easily seen for miles. Three separate arched entrances on the Broadway side welcomed the worshipers. From the entryway, four grand staircases led to the upper sections of the church. The wooden banisters were intricately carved, following Roeschlaub's ink-drawn designs. Two of the stairways led to the smaller corner towers, a third to the gabled belfry and the fourth to the sanctuary.

The slightly tinted arched windows in the sanctuary offered an amazing hue, lending to a glowing atmosphere in the enormous room. The ceiling of the room was suspended from a complex design of wooden rafters that sprang from the walls. Wooden pews, seating more than 1,200 parishioners, included delicate carvings. Elaborate carvings, again designed by Roeschlaub, also graced the arched frame of the wooden platform, which held an enormous Roosevelt pipe organ. Designed by G.A. Audsley of London, England, and built by the Hilborne Roosevelt Company in New York, the Roosevelt pipe organ is one of only twelve known Roosevelt pipe organs in the United States.

When the new church held its first service in early 1888, the congregation learned that the name had been changed to the Trinity United Methodist Church. Perhaps the most notable of the pastors was Henry Buchtel, chancellor of the University of Denver. A polished oak pulpit, highlighted with solid bronze, was later installed in honor of Pastor Buchtel, who went on to serve as governor of Colorado in 1907. Three years after the construction of the church, Robert S. Roeschlaub was recognized as Denver's leading architect by his colleagues.[14] In 1881, the Colorado chapter of the American Institute of Architects was formed, installing Roeschlaub as the first president, and he was continuously reelected to the office until 1911.

After seventy-five years, one of Denver's oldest churches received a renovation. During the process of cleaning the exterior, it was discovered that the Castle Rock rhyolite, discolored over the years, contained incredible hues of blue and red and a subtle glitter of mica. Another discovery after cleaning was the original embedded plaque, which read, "Trinity Methodist-Episcopal Church." (National Register, 7/28/1970, 5DV.115.)

In 1886, the Denver City Directory listed a new architect, William Lang. Through the directory, as well as several newspaper advertisements, Lang received work designing some of Denver's finest buildings. By 1889, William Lang and his new partner, Marshall Pugh, had been hired to design and build an astonishing thirty-five buildings. One of those was the St. Mark's Parish Church.[15] According to Denver architectural historians, while the religious edifice was indeed the "least modern" of Denver's churches, the same architectural historians praised the "brazen, exciting stylistic freedom" of Lang's work. Lang began the building of the church, located at the corner of Twelfth and Lincoln Streets in the heart of downtown Denver, in early 1889. Lang designed the house of worship implementing the High Victorian Gothic style of architecture, the first of three such styles erected in Denver. Constructed of soft gray limestone, the enormous structure stretched nearly a block. The High Victorian Gothic style, most evident in the exterior, included rounded pinnacles on either side of a four-story-tall square tower. Gothic arched windows graced every wall of the

When completed at Eighteenth and Broadway, the tall steeple of Trinity Methodist Church could be seen for miles. *Courtesy of Denver Public Library.*

church. The added or connected buildings—including the rectory, parish and offices—gave the appearance that the church was always growing.

The interior of the church, according to architectural scholars, "had many fascinating problems in scale." Another group of scholars, historians and professional architects agreed. In 1973, an observation of the interior of St. Mark's Parish Church by Historic Denver Inc. noted in part, "The smallness of the chapel, which is treated as parallel and analogous to the church itself, is made more apparent by the bigness of its buttresses. The size of the church is emphasized by elaborate small-scale aisles and side porches which separate it from the street. Tiny gothic windows which surround the church proper contrast with the much larger, more confident windows of the nave and northern apse. Large and small react to each other like color opposites in a painting: the small enhances the large, and the large, further diminishes the small."[16] Even so, Lang's design of the interior of St. Mark's Parish Church was simply stunning. The soft gray limestone walls were finished in rough-hewn Longmont sandstone, paneled oak and black ash trim. The sanctuary, with the many arched beams, lent to an open atmosphere. Even the architectural critics agreed, later writing, "Its spiky wooden beams, [and] weighty, clustered Romanesque columns hold up airy gothic arches. The rectilinear pattern of the exposed beams is visually exciting by the addition of gothic roundels which appear to swirl in free circular rhythm."

One of those "airy gothic arches" was created as the backdrop of the altar in the sanctuary, enhanced with seven thin vertical candelabrums. Years later, it became evident that the soft gray limestone used in construction was susceptible to Colorado's climate. This was borne out when the historic four-story-tall square tower slowly deteriorated and eventually fell in 1950. (National Register, 9/18/1975, 5DV.170.)

In 1890, Denver architect James Murdoch designed and built the All Saints Episcopal Church on the southwest corner of Wyandot Street and Thirty-Second Avenue in West Denver. Originally considered as a mission, Murdoch built the house of worship in the Victorian German style of architecture. Constructed of red brick and trimmed in natural stone, the many windows also received the same stone trim. The attractive entrance, centered under a beautiful round rose window, was constructed in contrasting pinkish brick with rough-faced stone trim. Inside, religious statues, all carved locally, were placed in rooms and hallways. The sanctuary, with its hammerbeam ceiling, also received a fair share of hand-carved wooden items. Along with the pews, the pulpit and baptismal base were also hand-carved.

Years later, the German Episcopalian congregation outgrew the church building and moved to a new location. Still later, the All Saints Episcopal Church was renamed the Chapel of Our Merciful Savior. (National Register, 6/23/1978, 5DV.132.)

Another notable Denver architect, Frank E. Kidder, designed the Christ Methodist Episcopal Church. Located at 2201 Ogden Street, Kidder built the house of worship in the Gothic Revival style using local sandstone. The gray-colored sandstone edifice was trimmed with red sandstone. The exterior of the church featured a corner bell tower. In 1927, the church was sold to a group of Methodists that renamed the religious edifice the Scott Methodist Church. (National Register, 11/7/1976, 5DV.127.)

Denver's Central Presbyterian Church has quite a history, dating to the earliest days of Denver's formation. In 1860, Reverend T.A. Rankin, considered to be the first Presbyterian minister in Colorado, arrived in the bustling mining supply town of Denver City. Rankin's detailed diary, housed at the Colorado History Center, reveals the reverend's disgust at the business dealings conducted on Sundays and the total disregard for the Sabbath. Nevertheless, Reverend Rankin persevered with his mission to organize a Presbyterian church for the newly recognized Pikes Peak region. The good reverend worked well with the leaders of Denver City and managed to recruit several leading citizens, including one of the town's founders, William Larimer; future judge Richard Sopris; and Richard Whitsitt. On a cold day in December 1860, Reverend Rankin walked to the office of the *Rocky Mountain News* to ask the publisher, William N. Byers, to publish a small piece announcing the formation and building of a Presbyterian church. As Reverend Rankin neared the newspaper office, he was caught in the crossfire of a shootout between an angry mob, Byers and local gambler Charley Harrison. Harrison saved both Byers and Reverend Rankin from harm.[17]

Two years later, in February 1862, Reverend Rankin dedicated a purchased lot on F Street, west of the gambling houses on the east side of Cherry Creek. The small red brick Central Presbyterian Church served the community for the next thirty years. In 1892, the Presbyterian congregation purchased eight lots at the southeast corner of Sherman Street and Seventeenth Avenue, for $40,000. One of Denver's leading architects, Frank E. Edbrooke, along with Willis Marean, designed the new Central Presbyterian Church.

Built in the Romanesque Revival style, the church was nearly square in shape and constructed of natural sandstone from the Redrock Canyon quarry in Colorado Springs. The carved exterior sandstone, with its red-orange color, was unusual to most Denver citizens. The roof of the three-story church was cross-gabled and included several chimneys. The dominant feature was the 136-foot-tall belfry. The high vertical thrust was emphasized by tall, thin lantern openings and capped with round arches.

While construction of the new church was underway, the Presbyterian congregation held services in the Broadway Theater. Evidently, the church members enjoyed the comfortable seating as well as the warmth the many fireplaces provided and let it be known. The sanctuary was built in such a way that it resembled an opera house. The cushioned seats were set in curved rows atop a sloping floor, allowing optimum visuals for all members. For added warmth, two fireplaces were built in the sanctuary, and others were strategically placed in various locations throughout the church. Beautiful stained-glass windows graced all three floors of the church, as well as intricate golden oak woodwork often featuring floral motifs. When completed in early December 1892, the total cost of the new Central Presbyterian Church was a hefty $250,000, an incredible sum of money in 1892. This was one of three of Edbrooke's last designs late in his remarkable career. Architectural historians consider the Central Presbyterian Church one of the most impressive of his public buildings.[18]

The new Central Presbyterian Church was dedicated in a ceremony on Christmas Day, followed by the first church service on that very holy day.

Through the years, the Presbyterian congregation was active in the community, from humanitarian needs to social causes. During the troubling political atmosphere of the 1920s, a time when the Ku Klux Klan infiltrated and dominated much of Denver's political offices, the leadership as well as the entire Central Presbyterian congregation stood in unity in opposition to the Klan and all the hatred that it represented, the first Denver church to do so.

Always concerned for the poor and downtrodden, the Central Presbyterian Church often opened its doors to the homeless on cold winter nights. Years later, a large portion of the church basement was opened as a shelter for the homeless, which it remains today. (National Register, 11/21/1974, 5DV.112.)

In 1898, Denver architect John J. Humphreys designed and began construction of Temple Emanuel/First Southern Baptist Church. Located at the southwest corner of Pearl Street and Sixteenth Avenue, the unusual style of architecture, with elements of Middle Eastern motifs, was considered the first such structure erected in Denver. Constructed of local beige-colored sandstone, the exterior also featured several elements honoring Judaism's Middle Eastern homeland. Three minaret-like towers with Turkish-style copper domes dominate the Pearl Street entrance. Two pavilions, one on the north side and one on the south side of the building, were also capped with copper domes. Floral motifs carved into the rough sandstone exterior were also an added feature. When completed in 1899, Temple Emanuel quickly became Denver's largest Jewish congregation.

In 1924, the popular congregation was able to expand with an addition to the building, erected by Humphreys's assistant, Thielman R. Wieger. The new addition, rectangular in shape, while following the Middle Eastern architectural style, also included several stained-glass windows, trimmed in native stone. The building housing Denver's first Jewish synagogue, Temple Emanuel, was eventually acquired by the City and County of Denver. Today, the historic building serves the Denver community as the Temple Event Center. (National Register, 11/25/1987, 5DV.715.)

In 1889, the small working-class settlement of Globeville was established. The residents, primarily Polish, worked at the smelters of the Globe Smelting and Refining Company. For the next two years, Globeville grew so much in size and population that the town was annexed to Denver in 1902. Shortly after annexation, the majority of Globeville residents gathered together at the St. Joseph's Society, Group 62 of the Polish Union of North America. By the end of that meeting, the St. Joseph Polish Roman Catholic Church and School Committee had been formed. The ethnic group believed that it was time they had their own house of worship such as the Germans' St. Elizabeth's and the Italians' Our Lady of Mount Carmel. Therefore, the group sent a formal letter to Bishop Nicholas Chrysostom Matz requesting his approval for such a church. Bishop Matz authorized the Polish community to raise the necessary funds for establishment of its own church and appointed Polish-born Father Theodore Jarzynski, a Holy Cross priest and graduate of Notre Dame, as the first leader of the new congregation.[19] Father Jarzynski stayed in the home of Frank Wargin during the construction of the church, conducting not only Sunday mass but often daily masses in the Wargin home.

Denver real estate developer James Tynon donated four lots in the 500 block of East Forty-Sixth Avenue for the new church. In July 1902, the architectural firm of Frank Kirchoff & Company began construction of the $2,000 church. Built in the traditional Gothic style, the red brick building included Gothic arched windows as well as the double doors at the entrance to the church. The distinguishing feature was the tall bell tower. Rising high above the central portion of the church, it was topped with a spire supporting a large cross. In December 1902, St. Joseph Polish Roman Catholic Church was completed, becoming the twelfth Catholic parish in

Denver. Bishop Matz dedicated the church during the first service, the Christmas mass of December 25, 1902.[20]

In 1920, Father Jarzynski was able to persuade officials of the Colorado and Southern Railroad company to allow his church the use of the original railroad depot, which had stood empty for years after the construction of a new depot. The depot was moved next to the church, at the northwest corner of Pearl Street and Forty-Sixth Avenue. For several years, this structure served as the St. Joseph Polish Roman Catholic Church School, where catechism classes were held. Because of the green-colored depot, the new school was affectionately known as the "Green School."

After twenty years of service to the church, Father Jarzynski died on June 14, 1922. Father John Guzinski, a Polish diocesan priest, became the second leader of the church. The following year, Father Guzinski was able to enlarge the church building through donations totaling nearly $3,000. In 1926, Father Guzinski also replaced the old "Green School" with a modern two-story red brick structure. (National Register, 4/21/1983, 5DV.782.)

Colorado's Bishop Nicholas Chrysostom Matz had envisioned a grand Catholic cathedral in Denver ever since his arrival in the city. To that end, in 1880 Bishop Matz formed the Immaculate Conception Cathedral Association. It would be thirty-two years before the bishop's dream would become a reality. Finally, following a European trip in 1901 during which he toured some of the finest Catholic cathedrals, Bishop Matz had new inspiration.

The bishop set about organizing a series of fundraisers, billed as the "Catholic Cathedral Building Fairs," which raised thousands of dollars.[21] Unfortunately, Michael Callanan, the rector responsible for the financial accountability of the organization, placed the money in a series of "investments" hoping to increase their coffers. One such investment was in a few lesser-known Cripple Creek mines that proved to be a loss. Callanan also invested a portion of the fundraised dollars in a new fad of funeral needs, such as glass-topped caskets. This also resulted in a loss for the association. Bishop Matz asked for and received Michael Callanan's resignation, appointing a new young priest, Hugh L. McMenamin, as Callanan's replacement. In the formal appointment, Bishop Matz wrote, "I hereby appoint you Rector of Cathedral parish. The time has come when the cathedral parish shall have to strain every nerve to build its grand cathedral. The people are willing and ready."[22]

One of Father McMenamin's first acts as rector was to reinstitute the fundraising efforts for the cathedral. In conjunction with Bishop Matz, Father

Mac, as he was affectionately known, was able to recruit John K. Mullen, a multimillionaire and avid Catholic supporter, to the Immaculate Conception Cathedral Association. Bishop Matz had performed the wedding ceremony of Mullen and his wife, the former Catherine Smith, in 1874. Mullen took a hands-on approach, becoming treasurer of the association. It was through his help, not to mention financial donations, as well as the efforts of both Bishop Matz and Father Mac, that the Cathedral of the Immaculate Conception finally became a reality. The Immaculate Conception Cathedral Association acquired eight lots at the northeast corner of East Colfax Avenue and Logan Street, the center of Denver's wealthiest neighborhood, Capitol Hill. Denver architects Aaron Gove and Thomas Walsh were hired to construct the new house of worship, designed by Detroit architect Leon Coquard. Designed and built in the traditional European style of Gothic Revival architecture, the building would take nearly ten years to complete. Because of the earlier fundraising scandals, Bishop Matz, Father Mac and John K. Mullen were all invested in the fiduciary responsibilities of the church construction. Mullen made regular visits to the site and sent his reports to Bishop Matz. In one such report, dated July 14, 1911, Mullen let his frustration and displeasure of the architects, Gove and Walsh, be clearly known:

> *The firm of Gove and Walsh have caused you and the Cathedral Association more trouble. They took Mr. Coquard's plans, did not put a scratch or a line on the plans. We had friction with Gove & Walsh from the very first day that work was begun under them as architects. Walsh never once went on top of the building until the day he went up on the tower. I myself begged him to go up with me. I climbed the ladder and Mr. Walsh didn't and he didn't hesitate to say that it was dangerous.* [23]

Nevertheless, construction continued nearly unabated. On August 7, 1912, just days before the church was completed, lightning struck the west spire of the building. Struggling to make repairs, the new Catholic house of worship was completed in October 1912.

The Cathedral of the Immaculate Conception was simply stunning. When placed in the Colorado and National Registers of Historic Properties in 1975, the property report noted that the "building is the finest example of Late Gothic Revival architecture in Colorado."

The building was constructed of gray sandstone and supplemented with granite from Gunnison, Colorado. Matching gray slabs of four-inch-thick limestone quarried in Bedford, Indiana, completed the rough-stoned exterior.

Notice the trolley car in front of the Cathedral of the Immaculate Conception. *Courtesy of Denver Public Library.*

The enormous structure was graced with many Gothic arched windows and doorways. However, it was the stunning feature of the twin towers that set the Cathedral of the Immaculate Conception apart from other Gothic Revival buildings in the state. Towering more than two hundred feet high, the sight was undeniably majestic. The east tower included a carillon of fifteen bells. Inside, religious art filled the walls and walkways, while Carrara marble imported from Italy graced the floors. The spacious sanctuary was

The incredible interior of the Cathedral of the Immaculate Conception. *Courtesy of Denver Public Library.*

dominated by a tall altar constructed of Carrara marble. Another stunning feature were the seventy-five stained-glass windows. The windows were designed by the F.X. Zettler Royal Bavarian Institute in Munich, Germany. When installed, the Munich glass firm claimed that twenty thousand pieces of glass went into the seventy-five windows. According to the archives of the Colorado Archdiocese, the Cathedral of the Immaculate Conception contains more stained glass than any other building in the United States. (National Register, 3/3/1975, 5DV.111.)

The greatest concentration of Denver's Italian immigrants settled in north Denver. Initially, these Italian families worshiped at St. Patrick's Catholic Church at the corner of West Thirty-Third Avenue and Pecos Street, as this was the only Catholic parish in north Denver at the time. However, the newcomers were not welcomed by the Irish communicants. Therefore, the Italian parishioners advocated for their own parish.

Father Joseph Carrigan, the Irish priest of St. Patrick's, also saw the need for an Italian priest for the growing Italian colony of Catholics in north Denver and urged Bishop Nicholas Chrysostom Matz to request such a priest. In response to the request, Bishop Matz sent for Father Felice Mariano Lepore. Father Lepore, originally from the southern Italy town of Cassano, Avilino, arrived in Denver from Pittsburgh, Pennsylvania, in 1891. From the outset, Father Lepore proved not only to be a strong community leader but also was extremely popular among his Italian parishioners. Early on, he became a champion for the poor Italian immigrants, many of whom were called "WOPS," which meant "without passports." The priest also founded a newspaper for the Italian community, *La Mazione*. One of his more notable achievements was the formation of the Mount Carmel Society, with the support of north Denver business leader Michael Notary. The Mount Carmel Society, with direction from Father Lepore, purchased seven lots in the Italian community for a new church. Shortly after, a new Italian Catholic church, a small frame structure, was constructed.

On Palm Sunday, March 18, 1894, Bishop Matz dedicated Our Lady of Mount Carmel Italian Catholic Church. However, a dark cloud loomed over the new church and its priest, as rumors followed Father Lepore, partially fueled by Italian husbands who distrusted the popular priest. Eventually, the rumors about the priest and women in his congregations were given some credibility when, in 1895, an ecclesiastical court found the priest guilty of "undue familiarity with women."[24]

Unfortunately, Denver's first Italian parish burned to the ground from an arson-caused fire. The *Denver Times* issue of August 17, 1898, reported that the fire left all of "Little Italy" in mourning. Undaunted, Father Lepore, along with the Mount Carmel Society, immediately began the construction of a new church. However, a rival Italian group, the St. Rocco Society, also had plans for an Italian church in the same area. Soon, an Italian Catholic rivalry was underway. Bishop Matz, who found himself caught in the middle of this rivalry, eventually refused to consecrate the Chapel of St. Rocco. Instead, he sided with Father Lepore, whom he had brought to Denver.

In late 1899, Bishop Matz consecrated the ground for the new church, located at the corner of West Thirty-Sixth Avenue and Navajo Street, with Father Lepore placing the cornerstone of the foundation for the new Our Lady of Mount Carmel Italian Catholic Church. However, it would be a few years before the congregation was able to raise the funds for construction of the new church. In early 1903, Denver architect Frederick W. Paroth, who had built St. Elizabeth Catholic Church in the historic Auraria neighborhood the previous year, was hired to erect the Italian house of worship. Construction at the southwest corner of Thirty-Sixth Avenue and Navajo Street began in February 1903. Paroth incorporated his expertise in the traditional European Romanesque Revival style in designing the building. It was an impressive structure. Built of brick, the building towered an astonishing one hundred feet and stretched nearly an entire block. The Revival design featured twin towers topped with four-sided copper domes. Above the front gabled entrance, a large window displayed a marble statue of Our Lady of Mount Carmel. A one-thousand-pound bell rang out from the tower of the church, which the parish also proudly called "Maria del Carmelina." The beautiful interior was enhanced with hand-painted Italian frescoes on both the walls and ceiling. Marble statues imported from Italy were placed in various sections of the church. While the doors of Our Lady of Mount Carmel were open to worshipers, the official dedication was scheduled for December 18, 1904.

In October 1903, two men, Joseph Guiseppe Sorice and Pasqual Gondosso, arrived in Denver with evil intentions. Sorice grew up in Cassano, Avilino, the same southern Italian town as Lepore, and had followed the priest to New York, Pittsburgh and then Denver. Lepore had been president of a bank that had failed in New York, and many Italians had consequently lost their savings. It was believed by investigators that Sorice was a depositor in the bank and never forgave Lepore for the loss of his savings. In Pittsburgh, too, Lepore had engaged in business and banking. Evidently, the two met at this Pittsburgh bank, and an argument ensued concerning the losses.[25]

Nevertheless, after Sorice and Gondosso arrived in Denver, Lepore confided to friends that the two men had tried to blackmail him. In an attempt to defuse their anger when they arrived in Denver, the priest gave them free rent in one of the residences he owned in the Italian community. On the evening of November 18, 1903, a drunken Sorice left a card game in north Denver and entered the priest's study at Our Lady of Mount Carmel

Catholic Church. There, Sorice shot Father Lepore three times. Somehow, Lepore managed to wrest the gun from his assailant's hand and shot Sorice in the abdomen. Sorice fell to the bottom of the cellar stairs with his head resting on a step. Father Lepore was able to stagger to the altar, where he laid his head on a pillow—perhaps for comfort, perhaps for spiritual guidance.

Both men lingered between life and death until the following morning, when authorities were called to the scene. Sorice died shortly after the police arrived. Father Felice Mariano Lepore died a few days later. He was thirty-five years old. On December 18, 1903, exactly one month after Father Lepore's murder, the rededication ceremony for Our Lady of Mount Carmel finally took place. Hundreds of proud Italians gathered for the procession led by Bishop Matz along Navajo Street. During the dedication festivities, Bishop Matz introduced the new priest to lead the parishioners. With Father Thomas M. Moreschini, the church was once again in good hands. (Colorado State Register, 5DV.709.)

Another house of worship designed and built by Denver architect Frederick W. Paroth is the historic St. Elizabeth Catholic Church, built in Auraria, Denver's oldest residential neighborhood. With such a large concentration of Germans in the area, Catholic bishop Joseph Projectus Machebeuf authorized the creation of Colorado's first German parish, St. Elizabeth Catholic Church. While Latin remained as the official language of the Catholic mass, Machebeuf also allowed the parishioners to conduct other church activities in their native German language. Bishop Machebeuf announced to his Catholic flock, "I have a Prussian exile priest to whom I have given the care of the Germans of Denver, and I have applied to the Franciscans for two priests to establish a house of their order and a parish here."[26]

The "Prussian exile priest" Bishop Machebeuf referred to was John Wagner. Father Wagner soon raised enough money to purchase two lots at the corner of Curtis and Eleventh Streets in the Auraria neighborhood. Construction for the new church began in 1878 and was completed within the year. Under the supervision of Bishop Machebeuf, St. Elizabeth Catholic Church flourished as Denver's German church and became the largest Catholic congregation in Denver. When the congregation had grown to such numbers that the church building could no longer accommodate its parishioners, the 1878 structure was torn down to make way for a larger, grander church.

In 1898, architect Frederick W. Paroth was hired to construct the new church at the same location, the street address of 1060 Eleventh Street.

The new church, measuring 130 feet by 69 feet, was built in the traditional European Romanesque Revival style, with elements of German Gothic as well. Natural native stone, quarried at Castle Rock, was used for the exterior and included tall arched windows and a large clock, as well as a bell tower. The dominating feature was the corner spire, which rose to 162 feet.

When completed, the total cost of the new St. Elizabeth Catholic Church was $69,000. Because of the generosity of Colorado's German Catholics, the church debt was paid off in a few short years. In accordance to church doctrine, once the debt had been retired, the new church could then be officially consecrated. On June 8, 1902, Bishop Nicholas Chrysostom Matz presided over the consecration ceremony. Sadly, a dark side of humanity would later cause the bishop to re-consecrate the church.

At the behest of Bishop Nicholas C. Matz, Franciscan fathers had agreed to handle the duties of the St. Elizabeth Catholic Church. Father Leo Heinrichs, of the Roman Catholic Franciscan Order, arrived in Denver on September 23, 1907, becoming the pastor of the St. Elizabeth Catholic Church. Father Leo Heinrichs would hold this position for five months until he would be murdered at the altar of this historic church.

Every Sunday, Father Heinrichs had conducted the 8:00 a.m. mass. However, on the Sunday morning of February 23, 1908, due to a meeting hastily scheduled for later in the morning, Father Heinrichs arranged to switch the mass duties with Father Wulstan Workman, who normally conducted the 6:00 a.m. mass, fondly referred to as the "Workingman's Mass." This particular mass was very popular, as it was a short sermon so that the men attending could arrive at their various places of employment on time. Father Heinrichs stood at the altar railing, offering the wafers and wine to the parishioners at the early morning hour. Fifty-year-old Giuseppe Alia, an unemployed shoemaker and known anarchist, was in attendance. Alia, carrying a hidden gun, moved to the altar along with the others for communion. When Father Heinrich offered a wafer to Alia, the self-professed anarchist spat the wafer into Father Heinrichs's face. Alia pulled his gun, aimed it at the priest and fired.[27]

As the bullet entered his chest, Father Leo Heinrichs staggered and then fell to the floor. Another early worshiper in the church that tragic Sunday was Denver police patrolman Daniel Cronin, who managed to jump over three pews in an attempt to reach the escaping assailant. Cronin finally caught him at the vestibule just as Alia reached the door. Alia turned his gun on the patrolman, but the quick-thinking officer inserted his thumb under the trigger.

Immediately, a crowd gathered and managed to surround the assailant outside the church. Many in the crowd cried out to lynch the murderer. Father Eusebius saved the perpetrator by appearing at the church entrance calling for silence. In the hush, he reminded the infuriated crowd that vengeance is the Lord's. While the priest held their attention, Officer Cronin pushed his prisoner into a carriage standing nearby, and the driver galloped to city hall. Meanwhile, Father Wulstan Workman arrived at the church. He could do nothing but administer the last rites. The bullet had pierced the left ventricle of Heinrichs's heart.

The *Rocky Mountain News* ran the following headline in its February 23, 1908 afternoon issue: "Assassin 'Hates All Priests' Father Leo Heinrichs, Pastor of St. Elizabeth's Catholic Church, Was Shot and Killed at the Altar This Morning by Giuseppe Guarnacoto Alia an Italian Anarchist, Who Entered the Church Ostensibly to Take the Sacrament."

The St. Elizabeth Church was closed after the coldblooded murder. The remaining Sunday masses were transferred to St. Mary's Catholic Church. Bishop Nicholas Matz ordered St. Elizabeth re-consecrated the next day so that a proper memorial and traditional wake honoring Father Leo Heinrichs could take place. The memorial was held on Wednesday, February 26, 1908. Nearly every priest in Denver attended the service, and the Knights of St. John served as the escort of honor, with the Knights of Columbus also in line.

In 1938, Father Leo Heinrichs's cause for beatification was opened. The proposal noted his charity, piety and spiritual leadership. The lengthy process was never completed, although attempts have been made throughout the decades, the latest being in 2010. (National Register, 12/1/1969, 5DV.128.)

By the 1880s, Colorado's high altitude, arid climate and abundance of hot springs locations were well known throughout the country as a natural cure, or at the very least relief, for "consumptives." A well-known physician specializing in the field of the tubercular condition, Dr. F.I. Knight of Boston, Massachusetts, wrote the following after a visit to the state in 1890: "It is a common saying in the East, 'If you go to Colorado for tuberculosis, you must live there forever after; you can never return to the East.'"[28]

During this period and up to the turn of the century, thousands of "consumptives" came to Colorado for their health and had few boarding options. Not only did most of the hospitals not want the patients, but many of the tubercular sufferers also did not want to be confined in a hospital. Thus, the majority of the consumptives found lodging in boardinghouses or hotels, as did Colorado's most famous tubercular patient, John Henry "Doc"

Left: St. Elizabeth's Catholic Church was the scene of a murder at the altar. *Courtesy of Denver Public Library.*

Below: St. Elizabeth's Retreat Chapel at Oaks Home. *Courtesy of Denver Public Library.*

Holliday. Holliday died in his room at the Hotel Glenwood in Glenwood Springs on the morning of November 8, 1887. Those with limited means remained in the Denver or Colorado Springs regions, where several private homes saw an opportunity to "provide care for the invalids."

The first such establishment of this type in Colorado was the Oakes Home. Reverend Frederick W. Oakes, an Episcopalian priest, arrived in Denver from Leadville in 1894. The reverend's sole purpose was to establish a home for use for the consumptive invalids of lesser means. Reverend Oakes later wrote that his mission was "[f]or that class of refined and cultured, although consumptive men and women who find it not an easy thing to secure healthful and congenial surroundings within their means."[29]

Reverend Oakes found the perfect property to further his mission. A large plot of land was purchased at the corner of West Thirty-Second Avenue and Eliot Street. Reverend Oakes first built the main building, known as "Hearts Ease," which accommodated one hundred patients. The Oakes facility accepted patients, charging eight dollars a week. Local physicians made daily rounds to the facility. As the Oakes Home became more popular, Reverend Oakes added buildings to the property. Of this period of expansion, Oakes described it as a "private home for tuberculosis [patients] who can not afford other arrangements and where a number of cases will be received for private treatment and supervision."[30]

By 1900, the Oakes Home was the largest of all such establishments in Denver. In 1903, Reverend Oakes hired local architect Frederick G. Sterner to build a chapel on the Oakes property. Sterner built the chapel in the elegant Classic Revival style. The porched entrance, with its four matching columns, included colonial windows topped with round rose windows. The centered bell tower was two-tiered and capped with a closed dome. Reverend Frederick W. Oakes served as the only chaplain for his St. Elizabeth's Retreat Chapel for the next thirty years.

In 1934, the Oakes Home closed. Years later, most of the buildings were demolished in the new fad of urban renewal of the 1970s. Fortunately, the St. Elizabeth's Retreat Chapel was left intact. In 1976, the chapel was one of the first historic properties to be listed by the Office of Archaeology and Historic Preservation. (National Register, 5/24/1976, 5DV.129.)

Father Joseph Projectus Machebeuf, the frail missionary from Santa Fe, New Mexico, had worked tirelessly organizing Catholic missions across Colorado Territory since his arrival in the southern portion of the area. In 1860, at the request of Territorial Governor William Gilpin, Father Machebeuf arrived in Denver City. Machebeuf and his companions arrived in the infant city on October 29, 1860. Machebeuf later wrote, "We were obliged to camp out on the 2 bare lots donated in Denver by the Express Co. having no neighbors but squirrels, prairie dogs and rattlesnakes. We walked around to see, not the city, but the little village of Denver, made up of low frame stores, log cabins, tents and Indian wigwams on the banks of the Platte."[31]

By the 1880s, Father Machebeuf, now a bishop, was instrumental in the forming of Denver's Catholic Annunciation Parish. Bishop Machebeuf had planned ahead for this event. Several years earlier, Machebeuf had donated a narrow tract of his ninety-acre farm to the City of Denver. Confined between the South Platte River to the west and the railroad yards to the east, the area was developed into the residential neighborhood known as St. Vincent's Addition.

In 1883, St. Ann's Catholic Church, the foundation of the Annunciation Parish, was constructed at the corner of Delgany and Thirty-Eighth Streets. The small red brick church was completed within the year. Bishop Machebeuf led the procession of parishioners into the new church, where he officiated at the dedication ceremony, culminating with the traditional act of sprinkling the holy water. However, in 1885, tragedy struck St. Ann's Catholic Church. As an unexplained fire quickly engulfed the building, the responding firefighters were blocked by a freight train.

Undaunted, the parishioners rebuilt their house of worship. In 1889, Father Henry Robinson became the leader of St. Ann's Catholic Church. In a bold, forward-thinking move, Father Robinson sold the church and the land for $7,000. With a portion of the profits, Father Robinson purchased land at a new residential development in northeast Denver. Located at 3601 Humboldt Street, the red brick structure was designed in the Gothic and Romanesque Revival styles and built by Denver architect Frederick Paroth. When completed in 1904, Father Robinson dedicated the church and named it Annunciation Church. (National Register, 6/21/1990, 5DV.3257.)

In 1904, the Episcopalians purchased a single lot on Clarkson Street, between Thirteenth and Fourteenth Avenues. No less than eighteen architectural firms submitted bids for the building project of a new Episcopalian church. In the end, the New York firm of Tracy & Swartwout was selected for the project. Its accepted bid proposed an English Gothic Revival style resembling Westminster Abbey in England, at a projected cost of $100,000.

Construction of St. John's Episcopal Cathedral began in early 1905 and would continue for the next six years. The exterior was built of dressed

Indiana limestone from the same Bedford, Indiana quarry as that of the Cathedral of the Immaculate Conception. The building was 185 feet in length and contained fifty-one stained-glass windows. Three arched doorways welcomed parishioners from the steps leading from the curbside. Twin towers graced either side of the north entrance, rising 100 feet in height. Fourteen chimes were installed in each tower, as were bells cast in Westphalia, Germany.

Inside, high ceilings, many as high as sixty-five feet, created an open atmosphere. The large sanctuary, which seated one thousand, included several hand-carved pieces of Salonica oak. Throughout the six years of construction, rising costs caused the architects to scale back from the original design. Nevertheless, as the new Episcopalian house of worship neared completion, the new Catholic building, the Cathedral of the Immaculate Conception, was also close to completion. Thus, a competition of sorts developed between the two, as each congregation wanted to be the first to open its doors. In 1909, the Catholics gained the lead when one of the pillars of St. John's Cathedral cracked in a lightning storm. Not long after that strike, lightning struck again—this time a tower of the Cathedral of the Immaculate Conception was damaged. It would be nearly nine months before the Catholic house of worship opened.

On November 5, 1911, the inaugural service was held for the Episcopalian worshipers. St. John's Cathedral represents the continuation of the first Episcopalian Parish established in Denver in 1860. (National Register, 8/1/1975, 5DV.171.)

St. Patrick Catholic Mission Church, located at 3325 Pecos Street in north Denver, was built amid swirling controversy and outright defiance. In 1883, Bishop Machebeuf authorized the construction of St. Patrick's Catholic Church. Located at 3233 Osage Street, the Romanesque Revival building built of red brick became the first Irish Catholic parish in north Denver. Two years later, Bishop Machebeuf approved Father Matz's appointment of Father Joseph P. Carrigan to lead the Irish congregation. Father Carrigan had arrived in Colorado in an effort to relieve his tubercular condition. When Father Carrigan assumed leadership of the parish, the church was already in foreclosure, unable to meet the $9,000 debt against the property. Father Carrigan actively encouraged the promotion of the Irish Celtic culture. He created and organized a parish festival celebrating St. Patrick. The Daughters of Erin, as well as the Ancient Order of Hibernians, joined Father Carrigan's celebration. The festival was so popular that it was repeated the following year, with added features such as an early morning mass, musical entertainment and a parade. The St. Patrick's Day Parade became an annual event, the first in Denver.

In 1906, Father Carrigan began planning a new church. The Catholic priest, returning from a trip to California, had been inspired by the many Spanish missions he had visited. The following year, Father Carrigan acquired a corner lot at the northwest corner Pecos Street and Thirty-Third Avenue. Father Carrigan worked with the Denver architect firm of Wagner & Manning, which designed the new building in the Mission Revival style. Unfortunately, for whatever reason, Father Carrigan failed to seek approval from his superior, Bishop Matz, nor did he consult with the Diocesan Building Committee.[32] When Bishop Matz learned of Father Carrigan's plans, he immediately ordered the construction stopped. Undaunted, Father Carrigan and his construction crew continued with their project. Thus, Bishop Matz dismissed Father Carrigan for insubordination. However, not only did Father Carrigan refuse to leave the parish, but he also requested the support of St. Patrick's board of trustees, as well as that of the Ancient Order of Hibernians. With their support and backing, Father Carrigan remained at the parish and the construction of the church continued.

Despite the inner Catholic controversy, by 1909 the exterior of Father Carrigan's new church had been completed. It was a mission complex including the church, a small library and a rectory connected by an arcaded walkway. Both buildings were constructed of smooth-dressed natural sandstone. Reflecting the Mission Revival style, the buildings were covered with red barrel tile roofs. Two tall square towers, capped with domes of painted sheet metal, graced the entrance. An inner courtyard was bounded by the three buildings.[33]

However, in June 1909, Bishop Matz sent a formal letter of dismissal to Father Carrigan. The letter, dated June 11, 1909, ordered Father Carrigan to refrain "from the exercise of all his sacerdotal faculties in the city of Denver, on account of grave disobedience."[34] Father Carrigan filed a lawsuit in Denver District Court. Bishop Matz retaliated by sending a statement to every Catholic parish in Denver and demanding it be read before the congregation. This statement declared that "the former pastor of St. Patrick's church in the city of Denver has incurred excommunication." For the first time in nearly four years, Father Carrigan complied with his superior's directive and read Bishop Matz's statement to his congregation, followed by his own statement of defense. By this time, not only were the local newspapers covering the growing scandal, the national media was carrying the story as well. Embarrassed by the scandal and the media coverage, the

Catholic apostolic delegate in Washington, D.C., launched an investigation and sent Archbishop Diomede Falconio to Colorado. However, it was John K. Mullen, a well-respected Denver businessman and a staunch Catholic, who intervened in the local matter. Mullen, who was good friends with both Carrigan and Matz, facilitated a meeting between the two men in which a compromise was achieved. Father Carrigan agreed to accept Bishop Matz's appointment as pastor of the St. Stephen Parish in Glenwood Springs, and Bishop Matz rescinded his excommunication decree.

For the next eighty years, St. Patrick Catholic Mission Church served the community. In 1989, the parish closed, and the Capuchin Poor Clare society of nuns acquired the property, opening the Our Lady of Light Monastery. (National Register, 11/14/1979, 5DV.109.)

In 1908, Denver architect Ralph Adams Cram designed and built St. Andrew's Episcopal Church. Located in the downtown area, 2015 Glenarm Place, the L-shaped building was constructed in the traditional Gothic style. Dark-red Harvard brick, enhanced with local limestone trimming, was the primary feature of the exterior. Gothic arches and a timbered ceiling were the dominant features of the interior. Diamond-paned windows composed of leaded amber glass graced both the interior and exterior. St. Andrew's Episcopal Church eventually evolved into a respectable teaching center for theological studies throughout the country. (National Register, 3/18/1975, 5DV.116.)

An example of an early twentieth-century urban neighborhood church was the Montview Boulevard Presbyterian Church, located in the Park Hill area of Denver. Built in 1910, no fewer than four architects participated in the project. Henry J. Manning and Frank W. Frewen, master architects and partners in the firm Manning and Frewen, designed and built the church in local rhyolite, following the Richardsonian Romanesque style. In 1918, Manning and Frewen constructed a small chapel on the property. In 1926, brothers Burnham F. and Merrill H. Hoyt, of the firm of Hoyt and Hoyt, designed and built a large educational wing, also in the Richardsonian Romanesque style. (Colorado State Register, 4/6/2003, 5DV.9034.)

During World War I, thousands of Slavic nationals fled their Austrian homelands for America's shores and freedom. In Denver, the Catholic Slavs worshiped at St. Joseph's Catholic Church in Globeville, at the behest of Bishop Matz. However, the Slovenians were charged a monthly fee of fifty cents for confession, as well as a "pew rental" of ten dollars per year. Following the death of Bishop Matz in 1917, the Slavic immigrants formed a committee to establish their own Catholic parish. This group of twelve men, all common laborers, traveled to Pueblo to meet with Father Cyril Zupan of St. Mary Slovenian Church, the only such congregation in the state. At a subsequent meeting, the group established the Holy Rosary Parish. A letter was then written and sent to Matz's successor, Bishop J. Henry Tihen, to appeal for their own Catholic house of worship. The letter, dated December 10, 1917, noted in part, "Slovenian and Croatian people of Globeville will regard permission to build their church as the best Christmas gift they have ever received or expect to receive."

The letter was signed by more than one hundred Slavic families. In January 1918, Bishop Tihen approved the creation of the Holy Rosary Parish. Anticipating a favorable approval, the Slavic committee had pooled their resources, $1,680, and purchased thirteen lots in the 4000 block of Pearl Street. Two members of the committee, Nicholas Shaball and John J. Yelenick, each donated a lot. Prominent Denver architect L.A. Desjardins designed and built the Holy Rosary Church. The brick building, measuring ninety-six feet by forty-six feet, was built in the Romanesque Revival style. Arched windows, as well as the arched entrance door, reflected the style, accented by an oval stained-glass window above the entrance. Twin bell towers, rising fifty feet, graced either side of the entrance. The interior of the church boasted no fewer than three altars. Several statues and religious art, donated by the faithful parishioners, graced the church. Completed in the spring of 1920, the total cost of construction was $35,000. The dedication of the church was delayed due to an early spring blizzard. Finally, on July 4, 1920, the formal Catholic dedication ceremony took place. Father Cyril Zupan, of Pueblo's St. Mary Slovenian Church, became the first pastor of the church. After a year of commuting weekly from Pueblo to Denver, Father Zupan requested that a new priest be assigned to the Denver parish. Solvenian-born Father John J. Judnic accepted the new assignment, arriving from Leadville on February 21, 1921. That same year, a $10,000 rectory was built that housed a library as well as living quarters for the first resident pastor. In 1927, the rectory became a convent operated by the Sisters of the Third Order of St. Dominic. (Colorado State Register, 3/10/1999, 5DV.349.)

The First Church of Divine Science was the creation of Nona Lovell Brooks, Colorado's first female minister. Born in 1861, Nona was the youngest of three daughters of Chauncey and Lavinia Brooks. After Chauncey Brooks lost his salt mine business, he relocated his family to the coal mining area of Pueblo, Colorado.[35] Several years later, Nona's older sister, Althea Brooks Small, met Kate Bingham, a follower and teacher of the New Thought philosophy, a type of metaphysical belief system that had developed in the late nineteenth century. In time, Althea persuaded her sisters, Fannie Brooks James and Nona Brooks, to attend Bingham's classes. Apparently, according to church history, on the third day of classes, Nona Brooks was "miraculously" cured of a painful throat ailment. Continuing with Bingham's classes, Nona witnessed several cures and became a firm believer.

Striking out on her own, Nona Lovell Brooks began teaching her own version of New Thought philosophy. A few years later, Brooks and Malinda Cramer, a California-based New Thought teacher, worked together, labeling their New Thought philosophy "Divine Science."

In 1898, thirty-seven-year-old Nona Lovell Brooks relocated to Denver, where she established the Divine Science College, a facility to educate teachers as well as ordain ministers in the philosophy of Divine Science. As an ordained minister, Pastor Nona Brooks commissioned the construction of the First Church of Divine Science in 1922. Denver architect J.J.B. Benedict designed the Classical Revival building, located at 1400 Williams Street. (Colorado State Register, 9/13/1995, 5DV.4689.)

In 1937, Denver's Lowry Air Force Base was established by the United States Military Department. Among the many structures typical of a military base, no fewer than four white clapboard chapels were built on the air force base. Building 27, as it was officially designated, was the first chapel on the base. Thus, the military-style chapel was also known as Chapel 1. Constructed in the cantonment style, as with the other structures, the lap-sided building boasted a tall steeple. The interior was a simple rectangular room with a long altar and rows of pews separated by a center aisle. When completed, the chapel was formally dedicated just two weeks before America was attacked by the Japanese at Pearl Harbor, Hawaii, December 7, 1941.

It was at this chapel that President Dwight David Eisenhower and his wife, Denver native Mamie Doud Eisenhower, attended church services when they were in Denver. During President Eisenhower's presidential term, the summers between 1952 and 1960 were spent in Denver, where Lowry Air Force Base served as the "summer White House."

During the Cold War, the military base continued to be used as an aviation training site until construction of the new United States Air Force Academy at Colorado Springs was completed. In 1982, several buildings at the base no longer in use were demolished. Building 27, or Chapel 1, was the only religious structure remaining on the base. It was during this time that the chapel was placed in the Colorado State Register of Historic Properties.

On September 30, 1994, the United States Air Force decommissioned Lowry Air Force Base. Two historic districts were created in the area: Lowry Technical Center Historic District and Lowry Officer's Row Historic District. In an effort to incorporate the chapel into the historic district, the building was actually moved in 2007. Under the supervision of architect Arthur Hoy, the chapel was raised and moved a mere forty feet to occupy the empty lot next to the newly created Lowry Officer's Row Historic District. With a grant from the Colorado State Historical Fund, the chapel underwent a renovation. The only change to the exterior was the removal of the steps to the entrance in an effort to make the building handicap accessible. The interior was also restored. A plaque was placed on the sixth pew on the left side of the chapel commemorating President Eisenhower and the First Lady's preferred seating during Sunday worship services. Today, the Eisenhower Chapel at Lowry, as it was renamed, is not open to the public, but visits can be arranged through the Lowry Officer's Row Historic District. (National Register, 5/6/1982, 5DV.193.)

In the southern end of the South Platte River Valley, the town of Littleton was established in 1861. In 1912, the Carmelite Convent was established with a unique history. It began with the marriage of Jacques B. Benedict and June Brown. Following the wedding, the couple bought an old red brick

Chapel no. 1 was renamed Eisenhower Chapel at Lowry Air Force Base. *Courtesy of Denver Public Library.*

The Carmelite Convent is located in Littleton. *Author's collection.*

farmhouse on the south shore of Ketring Lake and slowly began renovations. Benedict, an architect by trade, had received his training at the École des Beaux-Art Institute in Paris, France. Over the next several years, Benedict worked in transforming his property into a Beaux-Arts villa of sorts, while constructing many buildings in the Littleton community, including the Carnegie Public Library, located at the west end of Littleton Boulevard.[36]

Finally, in early 1912, Benedict hired a construction crew to carry out his detailed plans, which were based in Italianate elements. Artisans were hired to hand-paint frescoes on several walls, as well as the ceilings. Local landscape architect Saco R. DeBoer designed the grounds of the property. When everything was completed to Benedict's satisfaction, he and his wife named their home, appropriately enough, Benedict House. For the next thirty-five years, the couple enjoyed life at their house. Following the death of Jacques B. Benedict in 1948, the Benedict House was left to the Carmelites, an order of Roman Catholic nuns. The nuns maintained the former couple's home as living quarters and private studies. Improvements included a chapel with a matching red brick arch that connected with the original Benedict House. The Catholic nuns christened their religious retreat Carmelite Convent. (Colorado State Register, 5AR.510.)

CHAPTER 2

The Mountain Valleys

On that day his feet will stand on the Olives, east of Jerusalem, and the
Mountains will split in two from east to west creating a great valley, with half of
the mountains in the north and half moving south.
—Zechariah 14:4

Following the Pikes Peak Gold Rush of 1859 and Colorado territorial status in 1861, pioneer settlers moved westward, seeking their own fortunes in new beginnings, peace and prosperity. Although the winters in northern Colorado could be harsh, the high country of the mountain valleys often provided ideal areas to achieve those goals.

By 1860, the original route of the Overland Stage Company had been redirected. The route from Julesburg, northwest into Wyoming Territory, now ran along the northern front range of Larimer County. The new station for the Overland Stage Company was established by the notorious Joseph Jack Slade, the previous agent at the Julesburg station. Situated near Dale Creek, Slade named the new station "Virginia Dale," after his wife.[37]

While Slade continued to operate the new station in his usual tyrannical manner, Virginia Slade chose to bring civility to Virginia Dale. A Wyoming writer later noted of Virginia Slade, "Mrs. Virginia Slade, a lovely character, often interfering in her husband's business and many of the difficulties he had with people. His [Slade's] wife always possessed a great influence over him, even when he was drunk."[38]

Virginia Slade could indeed be forceful. Using her influence, Virginia insisted that church services be held on Sunday mornings. Although

Reverend Sheldon Jackson's legacy is reflected in many churches across Colorado. *Courtesy of Denver Public Library.*

Slade acquiesced to his wife's wishes, a building for such services was not built. By 1870, the Denver Pacific and Kansas Pacific Railroads had reached Colorado Territory. Not long after, the Virginia Dale stage station was abandoned. In 1872, westward settlers began moving into the area. Over the next few years, a close-knit ranching community existed. Although a formal town was never established, many of the old buildings were used for a variety of purposes, including a post office, a blacksmith shop and a general store. Later, a school was built and finally a church.

The Virginia Dale Community Church was built in 1880 on a portion of the Lilley Ranch land. A simple one-room log structure, the many windows along two sides offered natural light. Wooden pews faced the simple altar. A potbellied stove provided heat in the winter months.

In 1885, the church building was moved closer to the community, next to the local cemetery. Relocation of the small building took place at night. This was most likely done since it was the only time the local neighbors could spare their equipment as well as their time from their ranches. Later, the church received clapboard siding and was painted white. Still later, a steeple was built atop the roof and could be clearly seen for miles on the prairie.

Today, the Virginia Dale Community Church, along Highway 287, still holds Sunday services, weddings and funerals. It is on both the state and national lists of historic properties. (5LR.266.)

One of the seventeen original counties when Colorado became a territory in 1861 was Boulder County. It was named for the rocky creek that flows through the region and into the town of Boulder, which is the county seat.

Members of the First Methodist Church established a congregation in Boulder in 1859. It wasn't until 1891 that the church fellowship was able to erect a permanent place of worship. Architect Harlan Thomas was hired to build the First Methodist Church of Boulder. Located at the northeast corner of Fourteenth Street and Spruce Avenue, Thomas constructed the Romanesque Rival edifice at a cost of just over $22,000. A three-story tower, complemented by a pitched roof, graced the street corner. Ashlar sandstone,

Above: Virginia Dale Community Church is still in use today. *Courtesy of Kenneth Jessen.*

Left: Both the community of Virginia Dale and Virginia Dale Church were named for Jack Slade's wife, Virginia. *Courtesy of Denver Public Library.*

from nearby Green Mountain Quarry, was used in constructing the exterior of the structure. Contrasting limestone was used in the trimming of windows and arched doorways.

In 1960, Hobert Wagener was hired to construct a sanctuary, connected to the eastern portion of the church. Six gables of precast concrete were erected, complemented by a spectacular arched stained-glass window. (5BL.6242.)

The 1926 First Baptist Church of Boulder is perhaps the finest example of Late Gothic Revival architecture in the state. The building, which took two years to complete, included several elements of the style, including Gothic arched windows, doors and a steep pitched roof. (National Register, 4/14/2004; Colorado State Register, 3/10/2004, 5BL.6271.)

In 1870, several Swedish immigrant families established the small farming community of Ryssby. Located in Boulder County, the Swedish settlement lay about nine miles northeast of Boulder. In January 1878, the elders of the Lutheran Church of Colorado granted permission to the residents of Ryssby to build their own house of worship. It was to be named the Swedish Evangelical Congregation of Ryssby, Boulder County, Colorado.[39]

The Ryssby Church was begun by a Swedish settlement in 1881 in Boulder County. Note the outhouse to the left. *Courtesy of Denver Public Library.*

Today, the Ryssby Church, as well as the cemetery behind it, are still in use. *Author's collection.*

Services were held in the Ryssby schoolhouse until adequate funds could be raised for construction of a church. The first pastor for the newly formed church was Reverend Frederick Lagerman. In time, the congregation was able to purchase a 160-acre parcel, known as a *prastgard*, or pastor's garden. As was the Swedish custom, members of the church cultivated and farmed the land, raising a variety of crops, which were given to the

The interior of the historic Ryssby Church. *Courtesy of Ryssby Church.*

pastor as compensation for his spiritual leadership. In January 1881, one of the earliest settlers, Hugo Anderson, donated three acres of his hilltop farmland to build a church. Members of the congregation joined together to pool their talents in construction of the Swedish Evangelical Lutheran Church. Reverend Lagerman contracted with John Mork, a Norwegian member of the church, to build the structure. August Olander donated the sandstone from a ledge on his farm, where men quarried the stone and then hauled it to the construction site.

On Decoration Day 1881, members of the congregation held a ceremony for the laying of the cornerstone of the new church. As construction commenced, Charles Olson, a stonemason by trade, did the masonry work with the help of Andrew Lindberg, affectionately known as the "Swede Blacksmith."[40]

The square natural sandstone church included a high stone tower at the west end of the building. Lancet arches graced both the doors and windows. Finally, by the summer of 1882, the Swedish Evangelical Church had been completed. Dedication of the church took place on June 21, 1892, which happened to be Midsummer Day, a festive holiday in Sweden. Boulder County citizens from Longmont, Boulder, Niwot and Hygiene traveled to attend the dedication and first service, which was conducted in the Swedish language. Following the service, a second ceremony was conducted: the consecration of a cemetery near the churchyard, behind the church.[41] In 1914, the stone tower of the church was struck by lightning. A wooden tower was erected to replace the original. (National Register, 2/16/1984, 5BL.434.)

In the St. Vrain Valley of Boulder County, Edward S. Lyons established a quarry business on his land where the north and south forks of St. Vrain Creek meet. It was in this area that Lyons had discovered large quantities of red sandstone. In 1882, Lyons platted a town, the Lyons Township and Quarry Company. A few years later, as the small community grew, citizens came together to build a church.

Reverend Henry Harris, himself a stonemason, organized his fellow workers, as well as men from his congregation, to construct the new church. Located on the northwest corner of High Street and Fourth Avenue, construction of the First Congregational Church began in 1894. The foundation of the edifice was cut from a single block of sandstone from Lyons's quarry. The twenty-inch-thick walls were hand-cut from the same quarry. At the entrance, a square tower, forty-two feet tall, with an enclosed belfry, graced the exterior of the church.

Today, the First Congregational Church, affectionately known in Lyons as "The Old Stone Church," is one of the finest examples of stonemasonry from the quarry that benefited the town. (National Register, 12/12/1976, 5BL.357.)

Two years after the town of Hygiene was established in 1878, Jacob S. Flory, a German preacher with the Dunkard sect of German Baptists, built a church in the growing settlement. The Church of the Brethren, constructed in 1880, was built of native stone, with a simple gabled roof. The interior of the church included plastered walls, as well as a hand-hewn pine floor. At a total cost of $2,000, the church was completed within the year. The Church of the Brethren served the community of Hygiene until 1907. The cemetery, next to the church, continues to be maintained by the community. (National Register, 1/5/1984, 5BL.)

In the town of Longmont, established in 1872, the Episcopal congregation built St. Stephen's Episcopal Church in 1881. Although located on Longmont's Main Street, the area still remained largely undeveloped when the church was constructed. Therefore, St. Stephen's Episcopal Church was situated amid a splendid grove of spruce trees. The small church, built of local red brick, contained elements of the popular Gothic architecture, such as arched windows trimmed in stone. Inside, the inviting sanctuary provided plenty of seating. For the next ninety years, St. Stephen's Episcopal Church served the Episcopal community of Longmont. In 1972, the church was officially closed. Since that time, the building has been used in various commercial and retail ventures. (National Register, 2/24/1975, 5BL.355.)

In 1892, the Congregational Church was built in the town of Lafayette. The simple white frame church, built in Carpenter Gothic style, was financed by one of the town's founders, Mrs. Mary Miller. The steep pitched roof, with gables, supported the steeple. Unfortunately, the steeple was destroyed by weather in 1901. A porched entrance added to the charm of the quaint house of worship. The Congregational Church served the needs of Lafayette for several years, and Mrs. Mary Miller paid the minister's salary during that time.

Easter Services at Red Rocks Amphitheater have been a long-standing tradition. Here the author's great-uncle, Clarence Hoglund, plays the organ as he did throughout the World War II years. *Author's collection.*

The building also served as a meeting hall for the local coal miners, as well as a place for social gatherings. In 1918, during the Spanish influenza epidemic, the church building was transformed into an emergency hospital. By 1923, the town of Lafayette had purchased the building, which has served the community as a library ever since. (National Register, 5/20/1983, 5BL.821.)

In the gold mining town of Ward, established in 1863, the first church was built in 1894. The Ward Congregational Church, a simple wood-frame building, was actually built into the hillside with a side wall butted against the hill. The clapboard building, protruding from the hillside, featured a gabled roof that supported a bell tower. (National Register, 8/3/1989, 5BL.2672.)

Jefferson County, one of the original counties, contains many lush green meadows and valleys due to the streams flowing into the South Platte River. The town of Golden, nestled in the valley between North and South Table Mountains and Lookout Mountain to the west, became the county seat after being established in 1859. Golden also served as the territorial capital from 1862 to 1867.

Bishop George Maxwell Randall, the first elected Episcopal missionary bishop of Colorado in 1865, was instrumental in the founding and organization of Golden's first Episcopal church. In 1867, Bishop Randall commissioned John H. Parsons to build a chapel for the Episcopal school, Saint John's in the Wilderness. Following the groundbreaking ceremony and laying of the cornerstone by Bishop Randall, Parsons began the construction of the Calvary Episcopal Church.

Parsons built the church in the Gothic Revival style, which was "an introduction of this architectural style into Colorado."[42] The brick edifice included several Gothic arched windows. The steeple was supported by a sharply pitched roof. The simple interior included pews donated by Adolph Coors Sr., owner and founder of Coors Brewery, Golden's major industrial business. Among the earliest parishioners, including the Coors family, were Edward L. Berthoud, engineer and one of the founders of Golden, as well as William A.H. Loveland, also a town founder and owner of the Colorado Central Railroad. During the early years of the church, Loveland, who also served as treasurer, paid the shortfalls of the church's obligations from his personal funds.[43] In 1870, Mrs. George Jarvis donated funds for the construction of a corner belfry and bell.

In 1874, the Colorado territorial legislature approved the founding of a state school, the Colorado School of Mines, which included Bishop Randall's Saint John's in the Wilderness and the Calvary Episcopal Church. Today, the Calvary Episcopal Church is the oldest church in Golden. (National Register, 3/3/1995, 5JF.420.)

Not to be outdone by Bishop George Randall, the well-known pioneer Reverend Sheldon Jackson was instrumental in establishing the First Presbyterian Church of Golden. Land for the house of worship, at the southwest corner of Washington Avenue and Fifteenth Street, was donated by town founder William A.H. Loveland. James H. Gow used local sandstone and Golden pressed red bricks in the construction. The Queen Anne architectural style featured Gothic arched windows and doorways. A manse, constructed in matching materials, was erected at the south end of the church. A distinctive two-story square corner bell tower, completed with an onion dome roof, and an addition to the building were erected in 1898. A year later, the Courthouse Hill residential neighborhood was being developed around the church property. P.O. Unger purchased the lot south of the church, where he built a two-story Queen Anne–style residence in red brick. Not only did the red brick match the church edifice, but Unger also added a rounded corner tower to the Victorian home, which complemented the church's tower.

In 1958, the Presbyterian congregation moved to a larger house of worship. Two years later, in 1960, organizers of the Foothills Art Center

Reverend Sheldon Jackson was instrumental in building Golden's First Presbyterian Church in 1898. *Author's collection.*

purchased the church and manse, where they opened their gallery. In 1984, the Unger house was added to the gallery complex. (National Register, 3/14/1991, 5JF.418.)

Gilpin County, one of the original territorial counties of 1861, was named for the first territorial governor, William Gilpin. This small county, rich with gold, became the legendary "Richest Square Mile on Earth." With John H. Gregory's gold discovery in the waters of the north fork of Clear Creek, on May 6, 1859, the great Pikes Peak Gold Rush was launched. Mining camps sprung up along Clear Creek Canyon, including Black Hawk and Central City.

Into the busy, frenzied mining camp of Central City came the lay speakers and ministers of various Christian denominations. Among these men attempting to spread the word were Methodist preachers Jacob Adriance and William Goode, who arrived in July 1859. The two men had been recruited by the Methodist Conference, held in Kansas in June 1859, to travel to the Colorado gold fields. Both men readily agreed. Goode later wrote of his trip west as "a desire to strike one more blow for God and the Church in the regions beyond. Our arrival just when we did seemed to be Heaven-directed."[44]

Adriance and Goode preached at the cross intersections of Eureka, Main and Lawrence Streets every Sunday. In early July, Libeus Barney, an eastern reporter, had the occasion of witnessing a sermon given by Adriance and Goode. Barney later wrote of his observations, "The other corners on that intersection were occupied by those seeking life's temporal pleasures: on one, a 'grog shop' was dispensing whiskey, on one a 'soiled dove' solicited business and on one, a faro game was being disputed."[45]

Despite these nefarious obstacles, the two Methodist preachers were encouraged by local citizens. By August, Goode had organized the Methodist Episcopal Church. Thirty-five members attended the first meeting. Among those first members of the congregation were two of the city's most respected citizens, Henry M. Teller and Clara Brown. Teller was one of the first attorneys to arrive in the gold camp and quickly gained a reputation as a fair and honest lawyer. Clara Brown had made her way west after being legally freed by her southern master. Arriving in Central City, Brown earned her living washing miners' clothes and invested her money wisely in promising properties along the Front Range. During that first church meeting, Clara Brown generously offered her home on Lawrence Street as a meeting place for the new congregation.

For the next year, members of the Methodist Episcopal Church worshiped in the home of Clara Brown. As the congregation grew in number, Brown's small home could no longer hold everyone. During the summer of 1860, several men joined together to build a church. Located between Eureka and Nevada Gulches, a half mile from Central City, the log structure received the first worshipers on Christmas Day 1860. For the next year, services were held in the log church, until it burned in the winter of 1861.[46] Following the fire, Henry Teller used his influence with city and county officials to allow the Methodist Episcopal congregation to hold its Sunday church services in the courtroom of Washington Hall.

It was also during this time that the Annual Kansas-Nebraska District Methodist conference elected John M. Chivington as the first presiding elder of the newly formed Rocky Mountain District. Shortly after Chivington's arrival in April 1861, the *Central Christian Advocate* hailed the presence of Chivington and his fellow Methodist preachers. In an editorial printed in the April 10, 1861 issue, the editor praised the Methodist leaders:

> *What a field this is! And these hardy pioneers look as contented and happy as they can breath [sic]. Several preachers located as a necessity, others were transferred, but the body of them remained and all the vacancies were*

filled up with enterprising young men, and there were several applicants by men of families for whom there were no places. All the ranks were at once filled up, and the sturdy phalanx was then ready for any assault, however formidable.

One of the preachers arriving with Chivington was William Fisher, who became the first reverend of the Methodist Episcopal Church at Central City. The westward expansion of the Methodist Rocky Mountain District proved quite successful. By the following summer, the group had gained more than two hundred members, established fourteen preaching circuits and organized a dozen Sunday schools along the Front Range. At the annual Kansas-Nebraska District Methodist conference, it was decided that the 1865 conference would be held in Central City. However, there was no church. In January 1863, members of the Methodist Episcopal congregation pooled together and were able to purchase two lots on the steep corner of Eureka and County Line Streets. Then, a building committee was formed, led by Central City's respected attorney Henry M. Teller. The committee formed a building plan stating that the church would be built of "brick and natural stone." The *Central City Register* ran an editorial in the January 14, 1863 issue, stating in part, "The citizens here may well be proud. It is hoped that the church receives the support it deserves."

Cornish miners, who were also experts in masonry, were hired to help with the construction of the church. By February, construction had begun with the laying of the foundation. This was quickly followed by the erection of the stone walls.

During these early building phases, members of the church were holding fundraisers. In April, a public tea was held as a "nonreligious contribution" to the church. The *Central City Register* wrote about the upcoming event in the April 21, 1863 issue: "It is hoped that all those favorable to the cause of religion would try to attend. Admission, including tea, is fifty cents."

The fundraising tea event was fairly well attended, despite a heavy snowstorm. However, a storm of controversy soon erupted over how what few donations had been received were being used. Many citizens claimed that the funds were being used for the "present parsonage" rather than for the building of the church. Reverend William Fisher published a statement in the May 5 issue of the *Central City Register*: "Our books are open for investigation. We settle the Board of Trustees monthly, and do business on the square with all men."

And there the matter lay, quickly forgotten. However, in April 1864, construction abruptly stopped. It was discovered that the foundation was too shallow. Because of this, there was not enough ground support to hold the walls that had been erected. It is not known if Reverend Fisher was responsible for this construction error or if the tea scandal became too much for the church elders. In any case, thirty-year-old Bethuel Thomas Vincent was installed as the new reverend shortly thereafter. On September 11, 1864, Reverend Vincent, along with Henry Teller, presided at the ceremony where the laying of the cornerstone marked the new construction of the church. In his address to the crowd, Reverend Vincent said, "The cornerstone is laid for the erection of a church to the worship of almighty God, according to the usages of the Methodist Episcopal Church."[47]

Over the next two years, construction was slow, as various fundraisers did not bring in enough donations. Reverend Vincent, without approval of the church elders, was able to secure several small loans to continue with the building of the church. It is interesting to note that by the end of 1867, Reverend Vincent had been replaced by Reverend George Adams. The new reverend was able to enlist the Cornish miners among his congregation to donate their time and labor to the construction of the church.

Meanwhile, Reverend Adams, after learning of the high interest rate on the loans and the severe debt the church was in, penned an open letter published in the *Central City Register*:

> *This building was begun through the influence of a man who was a member of the church and supposed to be wealthy, on a scale that the judgment of the congregation did not approve. He assured them of success, however, and promised to lift it out of all financial difficulty. This man failed, left the country and took the benefit of the bankrupt law, leaving a debt of $2,000 at 3 percent interest per month which reached the sum of nearly $5,000 by the time the work was resumed.*[48]

By November 1868, the exterior walls had been erected and the basement completed. Under Reverend Adams's leadership, the Methodist Episcopal Church held its first church service on the first Sunday of January 1865. Services, held in the basement, began at 11:00 a.m., followed by communion and a children's concert.

Nevertheless, the church was without adequate funds to complete the construction. While the congregation continued to hold its Sunday services in the basement, fundraising also continued. In 1871, M.H. Root,

Left: St. James Methodist Church in Central City was built in 1863. *Courtesy of Gilpin County Historical Society.*

Right: Today, the St. James Methodist Church still serves the community of Central City. *Courtesy of Linda Jones.*

a local stonemason, was hired to complete the building of the church. Complementing the original stone structure, Root added a flat-squared bell tower. Root installed arched windows as well as an arched entrance. After nearly ten years, the exterior was finally completed. Inside, stenciled wallpaper graced each side of the sanctuary, where spectacular stained-glass windows had been installed in October 1871. When the magnificent walnut pews were placed in the sanctuary the following month, the church was ready for its worshipers. The total cost for construction of the church was $42,000.

The first services were held in the sanctuary in November of that year. However, the dedication service for the Methodist Episcopal Church was celebrated the following summer. Denver's Methodist bishop, R.H. Foster, traveled to Central City to conduct the dedication ceremony on July 21, 1872. In 1899, a rare Steere & Sons pipe organ was installed in front of the sanctuary. This organ operated by water power until modernized in 1932.[49] (Colorado State Register, 5GP.511.)

In 1859, after George Jackson discovered gold at Payne's Bar, a mining camp soon sprang up known as Idaho Springs. When the Colorado Territory was formed in 1861, Clear Creek County was established, with Idaho Springs serving as the county seat. The Methodist Episcopal Church was constructed in 1880. The Gothic-style building, built of red brick, featured arched windows and a steep pitched roof with a belfry attached off to one side. As the congregation grew over the years, two additions were added to the church. Today, the historic church stands empty, a ghost of a happier time. (Colorado State Register, 5CC.241.)

A year after Jackson's gold discovery, the Griffith brothers, David and George, discovered a rich silver vein at the base of what would later be named Griffith Mountain. After filing their Griffith Lode mining claim, the brothers formed the Griffith Mining District, and later the mining

Grace Episcopal Church in Georgetown. *Courtesy of Denver Public Library.*

town of Georgetown, named for George Griffith, was established. In 1867, Reverend William Winslow of Black Hawk arrived in Georgetown to lead a congregation of Episcopalians in fellowship and prayer. Inspired by Reverend Winslow's visit, the Georgetown Episcopalians spent the next two years raising funds to construct a church. One of the members of the congregation, a woman named Grace, was instrumental in this fundraising process. In 1869, a lot was purchased on the east side of Taos Street, where the foundation of the new church was laid.

The Episcopalian congregation unanimously agreed to name its new church Grace Episcopal Church, in honor of its dedicated member. This church would become the first Episcopal church erected in the state.

Cornish miners were hired to build the church, which rested against the side of a steep hill. Constructed in the Carpenter Gothic style, the exterior of the building featured the traditional clapboard siding, with accented wood trimming around the arched windows and double doors. The pitched shake-shingle roof included front gables and was topped with a bell tower. The interior of the church featured an open-truss roof structure and hand-carved wooden pews.

The interior of Grace Episcopal Church. Note the Johnson pipe organ. *Courtesy of Denver Public Library.*

Unfortunately, shortly after the new church was completed, fierce mountain winds on Thanksgiving Day 1870 caused portions of the church to fall. Undaunted, the congregation worked together and reinforced the church using tie rods, replaced the windows and repaired the church's wooden trimming. The bell tower, which had been knocked off the roof, was redesigned and placed beside the church.

In 1877, the church acquired a Johnson pipe organ. The rare pump organ, in its solid oak casing, is believed to be the oldest operating pipe organ in the state.[50] The organ was later electrified and is still in use today. In 2006, Grace Episcopal Church received the Stephen H. Hart Award for historic preservation.[51] (Colorado State Register, 5CC.582.)

Not far from the Grace Episcopal Church, also on Taos Street, the First United Presbyterian Church was erected in 1874. Reverend Sheldon Jackson, the Presbyterian missionary, organized the local Presbyterians and held the first meeting in the Methodist church. As the congregation grew, Jackson held fundraisers in an effort to build a church. In 1872, a lot overlooking Clear Creek was purchased, and construction of the First United Presbyterian Church of Georgetown was soon underway. Natural unfinished granite was used in the Gothic-style structure. Pointed arched windows were trimmed with red brick, as were the two arched doorways. A steep pitched roof covered the main portion of the church. At the northwest corner of the building, a two-story square bell tower rose to the same height as the main roof. The arched Gothic windows on the tower matched those of the main building. At the top of the bell tower, a wooden turret, painted white to match the wooden doors, was capped on all four sides with eight pinnacles. The interior of the church, with its rough granite walls, blended with the rustic mountain atmosphere. The wooden pews were placed in long single rows on one side of the room, leaving a walkway to the altar on the opposite side.

The regal interior of the First United Presbyterian Church in Georgetown. *Author's collection.*

When completed in 1874, the total cost to the congregation was $7,000. The first service included a dedication ceremony held on September 20, 1874.

In 1974, the Presbyterian congregation celebrated its centennial anniversary. The members also took this time to renovate sections of the church. Unfortunately, one of the renovation projects entailed the remodeling of the church's interior. White plaster was placed over the natural granite walls as well as the ceiling. The arched windows received new frosted glass. The new whitewashed look replaced the original rustic atmosphere that was so unique to this historic church. Nevertheless, today the First United Presbyterian Church remains Georgetown's only church to maintain continuous services since 1874. (Colorado State Register, 5CC.582.)

Georgetown's First United Presbyterian Church was built in 1874. *Courtesy of Denver Public Library.*

For more than 140 years, the First United Presbyterian Church has served the community of Georgetown. *Author's collection.*

Not to be outdone, at the same time the Presbyterians were building their house of worship, the Catholics were building a new church. The original Our Lady of Lourdes Catholic Church, a small clapboard structure at the north end of the town, had quickly outgrown its parishioners. The new church, also located on Taos Street, in the block between the Grace Episcopal Church and the First United Presbyterian Church, was completed in 1875.

The new church, built of brick, included arched windows and doors and was topped with a centered belfry above the entrance. At a cost of $12,000, the grounds surrounding Our Lady of Lourdes Catholic Church were a complex including a rectory, a school and a hospital. In 1917, the church complex burned to the ground. The following year, the Catholic congregation was able to acquire the Methodist church property. Within the year, a fine new brick church was built. (Colorado State Register, 5CC.582.)

Two miles west of Georgetown, the mining camp of Silver Plume was incorporated in 1880. However, before formal incorporation, the residents had taken it upon themselves to build not one but two churches in their

Our Lady of Lourdes Catholic Church in Georgetown. *Author's collection.*

mining community. Both churches were later moved from their original locations, one of which was literally lifted skyward.

The first was St. Patrick's Catholic Church, most likely due to the large population of Cornish and Irish Catholic miners. Located on Silver Plume's

Main Street, construction began in 1872. The Cornish miners built a stone foundation nearly one foot thick for the church. An A-frame wooden building was constructed atop the foundation, fashioned in the traditional Gothic style of architecture. The typical arched windows were placed on all sides of the building. A tall wooden stand was built atop an elevated stone platform, which held the church bell.

In 1884, fire swept through the town, effectively destroying more than half of the buildings. Fortunately, the Catholic church was spared from destruction, although the east side of the building was severely scorched. Not only was the damage repaired, but the entire building was also lifted off the foundation, turned ninety degrees and replaced on the foundation. As the congregation grew, plans were agreed on to expand the church. In 1886, the *Georgetown Courier* ran several announcements in various issues of the paper: "The Catholic Church at Silver Plume will be enlarged to accommodate the constantly increasing congregation."

Later, in 1886, the new addition to the church was built with the front facing Main Street, while the original structure served as the rear vestry. Above the arched doorway, a round window featured a rose in the stained glass. Inside, the walls of the church were decorated with extraordinary stenciled drawings. In 1898, hand-carved double wooden doors were imported from Italy, gracing the clapboard addition.

The Silver Plume Catholic Church continued to serve the community for more than 120 years. However, due to the economy and the increasing maintenance costs, the church was finally closed. Today, it is privately owned. (Colorado State Register, 5CC.582.)

A few years after the Catholic church had been built, the Methodists in the area built their own house of worship. The church was originally built in the small mining camp of Brownville, located a half mile west of Silver Plume. The Methodist church, an A-frame wooden structure, was built very near the base of Brown Mountain. Above the double-wide door, a square belfry was constructed off to one side of the pitched roof. As Silver Plume grew in population, the town moved westward, eventually overtaking the mining camp of Brownville. In 1890, following years of snow and mudslides, the Methodist church was moved to a site on Hancock Street in Silver Plume. (Colorado State Register, 5CC.582.)

Another of the original seventeen Colorado Territorial counties, Summit County was created due to its vast mineral wealth. Breckenridge, the county seat, was named for Vice President John C. Breckinridge, but the spelling of the surname was altered just a month later when it was

The Silver Plume Catholic Church still stands above the main street in the mining town. *Courtesy of Denver Public Library.*

learned that he had enlisted with the Confederate army when civil war broke the nation in two.

Methodist minister "Father" John Lewis Dyer traveled throughout the many mining camps of Colorado, preaching the gospel to all who would listen. In 1860, Dyer arrived in the mining settlement of Breckenridge. Dyer later wrote of the experience in his journal:

> *Friday, July 6, 1860—With a shirt in one pocket, a Testament and hymn-book in the other, bread and beef in a third, I started out on foot for Blue River, crossing the Snowy Range at what is called "Boreas Pass," arriving at Breckenridge at night. On Saturday I found some Methodists. I*

preached on Sunday at four P.M., The [next] *Sunday I preached at Blue River, organizing a Class* [sic] *of six members, and at Breckenridge in the afternoon, formed a Class of seven. The Lord was with us to bless. This was the beginning of Methodism on the Pacific Slope of Colorado.*[52]

That same year, Father Dyer, along with trustees of the Methodist Episcopal Church Thomas Bonney, A.J. Floyd, John S. Reid, B.R. Smith and Andrew J. Thompson, executed a quit-claim deed with the officials of Breckenridge. The deed, at a cost of one dollar, gave them title to a sixty-foot lot, on which they intended to build their church.

A local carpenter, E. Bruce Schock, designed and built the simple clapboard one-room structure atop a log foundation on French Street. Rectangular windows were neatly placed on each side of the church, and double doors welcomed the worshipers. Three years after construction, a local newspaper printed an editorial concerning the somewhat plain-looking church: "The Methodist Church on French Street, the first built, was erected in 1880. In addition to being in an obscure position it is overshadowed by the large Fireman's Hall beside it so that a stranger would have to come directly in front of it before he would realize it was there."[53]

By 1881, Father Dyer had resumed his preaching, traveling to various settlements on the western slope. Reverend J.F. Coffman became the second leader of the Methodist church. Reverend Coffman built a one-

Father Dyer was instrumental in the building of this church in 1860. Through the years, additions were constructed. Today, it is known in Breckenridge as the Father Dyer Methodist Church. *Courtesy of Denver Public Library.*

story log building that served as a parsonage. During his three-year tenure as the church leader, Reverend Coffman made great strides in bringing new members into the fold. However, the meager salary was not enough to live on. In 1884, the reverend left the church and Breckenridge for greener pastures. Father Dyer returned to take Reverend Coffman's place, later writing, "The unsettled condition of mining camps is unfavorable to the keeping up of religious societies."[54]

In 1888, Father Dyer caused a bit of apprehension in Breckenridge, raising the ire of many. Although Father Dyer had received permission from city officials to use the fireman's bell on Sundays, it quickly became a source of contention among the volunteer firemen, not to mention the town's citizens. When Father Dyer rang the bell that first Sunday, the volunteer firemen rushed to the firehouse only to learn that bell ringing signaled the beginning of the Methodist service. The citizens were unnecessarily frightened, thinking fire had broken out in the town. The *Summit County Journal*, in an editorial, blasted both the city officials and Father Dyer. At the end of the piece, the editor asked one question: "Yesterday the Fireman's Hall bell tolled as usual for the church service; who is on top, the Town Trustees or Father Dyer?"

Apparently, the problem persisted, forcing the firemen to move their building down the hill to a lot on Main Street. During the move, damage was done to a portion of the church, which stood next to the fire hall. The *Summit County Journal* reported the incident in the June 30, 1888 issue: "The corner of the M.E. Church that was injured by contact with the Fireman's Hall when the latter was removed last winter is still in its shattered condition. The contractors who removed the hall should have repaired the damage done long ago, but it is not too late yet."

In 1889, a new pastor came to the Methodist church, Florida Passmore. Reverend Passmore, young and energetic, quickly brought needed changes to the church. Not only did Passmore spruce up the interior of the church, but he also persuaded the congregation to contribute funds for its own bell and a belfry to house it. Reverend Passmore fought tirelessly for passage of a state law that would require saloons to close at midnight and remain closed on Sundays. When the law finally passed, the miners in the Breckenridge area held Reverend Passmore responsible. On the night of Monday, August 17, 1891, the belfry of the Methodist church was dynamited. While the congregation was devastated by the deliberate destruction, Reverend Passmore seemed undaunted. He continued to rail against the saloons. Over the next few years, Reverend Passmore became more radical in his actions.

Shortly thereafter, the leaders of the Colorado Methodist Church voted to dismiss Reverend Florida Passmore from the ministry.

In 1904, another energetic pastor took the helm of Breckenridge's Methodist Church. Reverend W.A. Pratt set out to improve the tarnished image of the church, both internally and externally. The *Breckenridge Bulletin* reported on the work of Reverend Pratt in the Saturday, July 8, 1905 issue: "It has recently developed that Rev. W.A. Pratt is an expert with the saw and plane. He has greatly improved the M.E. Church. The vestibule front door of the church has folding doors leading to the street, and the church edifice is now receiving a coat of paint, making the place decidedly attractive. Rev. Pratt can work as well as preach."

During World War II, many of Breckenridge's buildings fell into disrepair, including the Methodist church. In 1966, the church was again renovated and a new addition built. Under Reverend Mark Fiester, the church was renamed the Father Dyer Methodist Church. Reverend Fiester commissioned a stained-glass window that depicts Father John Lewis Dyer, the "Snowshoe Itinerant," on his infamous handmade Norwegian-style snowshoes.

Ten years later, during routine maintenance, it was discovered that the original log foundation of the church had rotted. By the following year, 1977, efforts were underway to move the building to a new location. The board of trustees was able to purchase a corner lot at Briar Rose and Wellington Streets for $7,000. On June 25, 1977, the Father Dyer Methodist Church was placed safely on its new foundation in its new location. When the work had been completed, members of the congregation proudly rang the church bell.

Not long after Father Dyer and the Methodists built their church, the local Congregationalists worked together to build their own. The small clapboard edifice, with a steep gable roof, included an open belfry. Unfortunately, the Congregationalists were a small group and were unable to keep up with the costs of the building.

In 1881, the Episcopalians purchased the church for $300. The building was then moved to French Street, just a few doors from the Methodist church. From that location, the new St. John the Baptist Episcopal Church was home to the Episcopalians.

While the Episcopalians were setting up their new church, the Catholics were building their house of worship, St. Mary's Catholic Church, on the southeast corner of High and Washington Streets. Father Thomas Cahill enlisted the help of his parishioners to erect the building, which was completed in ten days. Built in Carpenter Gothic style, shingle

The interior of Father Dyer's original church. The structure is now located in South Park City. *Author's collection.*

siding complemented the roof of this otherwise plain-looking church. The interior was tastefully done, with hand-stenciling on the walls and ceiling. However, Father Rhabanus Gutmann, a German monk, detested the new Catholic church, saying that St. Mary's was "a disgrace to the name of St. Mary."[55]

In 1899, an open belfry was erected with four pedimented gables and shingle siding. During the economic depression of the 1890s, the church building was moved to the northwest corner of Washington Street. There, Benedictine monks were instrumental in creating the St. Joseph Hospital, as well as the St. Gertrude's Convent and Academy. Both institutions stood next to St. Mary's Catholic Church.

Garfield County was created in 1881, the year President James A. Garfield was assassinated. Two years later, the resort town of Glenwood Springs became the county seat. The first, and hence the oldest, church in Glenwood Springs was constructed in 1886. The First Presbyterian Church was built on a stone foundation quarried locally. The interior was bright with sunshine from the many windows, and the large rafters supporting the roof lent to an open atmosphere. Renovations and additions were added in 1949. (Colorado State Register, 5GF.)

In 1889, Rio Blanco County was created amid the White River Valley of Colorado's western slope. The White River, as it was referred to by the white man, was known to the Ute Indians as the Smoking Earth River. It was in this area that Indian agent Nathaniel Cook Meeker was murdered in 1879 during a Ute uprising at the White River Indian Agency. The town of Meeker, named in honor of the slain Indian agent, became the county seat.

In 1885, a few local settlers in the White River Valley came together to establish a new town. With the leadership of William H. Clark, John C. Davis, J.W. Hugus, Newton Major and Susan C. Wright, the town of Meeker was incorporated. Many of the buildings that were not destroyed by fire during the Indian raid at the White River Indian Agency were sold by the government to the town founders for $50 each, with $100 for the officers' quarters. These structures were moved to the fledging town.[56] For the next twenty years, the town of Meeker remained the only incorporated town in northwestern Colorado. The same year that Rio Blanco County was created, Reverend Arthur Williams arrived in Meeker. Within a year, Williams had organized the local Episcopalians, held fundraisers for a church and raised more than $600. In 1890, Reverend Williams, along with members of the congregation, dug the foundation and laid the cornerstone for their St. James Episcopal Church. Located at the corner of Park Avenue and Fourth Street, the church was built in the traditional Queen Anne style. Local rough sandstone, quarried near Flag Creek, was used for the exterior, accented with buttresses of lighter sandstone. The spectacular bell was a product of the Blymer Bell Foundry of Cincinnati, Ohio.

After ten years with the St. James Episcopal Church, Reverend Arthur Williams became a bishop and was transferred to Nebraska. Then, in 1908, Reverend Williams was in Washington, D.C., as an Episcopalian representative for the cornerstone-laying ceremony for the new Episcopalian cathedral in that city. After the ceremony, wherein Reverend Williams had spoken a few words, President Theodore Roosevelt, who was also in attendance, requested a private meeting with Bishop Williams. During a few of Roosevelt's many hunting trips in Rio Blanco County, Roosevelt had attended church services at the St. James Episcopal Church in Meeker. During the meeting, Roosevelt is reported to have said, "I know all about you, the people up there haven't quit talking about that man Williams who did things out there in the early days. I'm mighty glad to meet you, Sir."[57]

In 1931, Reverend W.O. Richards became the leader of the St. James congregation. One of his first tasks was to find a way to replace the cross that had fallen from the top of the bell tower. In due time, the good reverend found a way to replace the cross, but he never disclosed his methods. Years later, Mrs. Richards recounted the incident:

> *There was a farmer, a Roman Catholic, who was a sheet metal worker. He came to my husband and said he knew where he could get copper to cover the cross and to replace the rotted wood in the church tower so that the bell could be hung there without falling through the roof. It was at the time of the Prohibition years and this person knew where was a liquor "still" and could get the copper there, but this was to be kept a deep secret, which was kept. He did the work free of charge. Now since all concerned have passed to their reward, the secret can be told.*[58]

The St. James Church is listed in the National Register. (3/30/1978, 5RB.983.)

Named in honor of Governor Frederick W. Pitkin, Pitkin County was created in 1881. The new county, high in the heart of the Rocky Mountains, included some of the state's richest silver mines. With so many mining claims scattered throughout the mountain region, small mining camps such as Ashcroft, Independence and Ute City sprang up.

The mining camp of Ute City, named for the friendly Ute Indians in the region, was created during the Pikes Peak Gold Rush of 1859. During that first winter, several of the miners laid over for the winter to guard their claims. The following spring, as new miners arrived, the mining camp took on a semblance of organized settlement. As Ute City quickly grew in size and population, nearly three hundred, the mining camp was renamed Aspen for the colorful trees. Aspen became the county seat. Reverend H.S. Beavis arrived in Aspen shortly after the congregation of the First Presbyterians had been formed in 1886. Within four years, under Reverend Beavis's leadership, a town lot at the northeast corner of Aspen and Bleeker Streets was purchased in 1890, where the construction of the First Presbyterian Church began. Built of local rough-faced red sandstone, quarried at the Peach Blow quarries in the Frying Pan River Valley, the three-story edifice was designed in the Romanesque Revival style, which also included many aspects of the Queen Anne style of architecture. The entrance, with its double doors, was flanked on either side by three-story towers. An enclosed bell tower was capped with a bell-shaped shingled roof. The 1975 Colorado Historic Preservation assessment described the exterior: "Somewhat fortress like in overall appearance, the facade is dominated by a large corner bell tower that is cylindrical in form and topped with a bell shaped roof. Gables extend from the steeply pitched roof."

Inside, church offices, meeting rooms and classrooms were on the main floor. The sanctuary, located on the second floor, featured hand-carved semicircular pews seating 350 worshipers. Stained-glass windows were completed, with detailed woodwork in the window frames. When completed, a year later, the total construction cost was $30,000. A short time later, *Harper's Weekly* ran an article on the virtues of Aspen, which in its view "had been noted from the start." The piece went on to describe the exterior of the First Presbyterian Church: "Its lines epitomized the unyielding respectability and force of character that is Aspen."[59]

In 1920, the local congregation of United Methodists joined the Presbyterians. Ten years later, the two religious groups agreed to rename the church the Aspen Community Church. (National Register, 5/12/1975, 5PT.33.)

Aspen's First Presbyterian Church was built in 1886. *Courtesy of Denver Public Library.*

In 1877, the year following Colorado statehood, Governor John L. Routt signed legislation creating Routt County, named in his honor. The ranching community of Steamboat Springs became the county seat.

The high country of Yampa Valley was ideal ranch land, yet winters were harsh and the residents isolated. Permanent settlers were few until James H. Crawford brought his family in the spring of 1875 to the area of the ancient spring waters, where they occupied an abandoned log cabin near Sulphur Spring. Crawford believed so much in the area that he laid out a townsite, which he named Steamboat Springs for the chugging sound of the natural springs in the area.

Those who settled and stayed considered skiing a way of life. During the winter, cross-country skiing was a Sunday family and social affair. Families, including the toddlers, skied to the stone quarry of Emerald Mountain, south of Steamboat, enjoyed a picnic lunch, played in the powder snow and skied back to their homes by late afternoon. Strawberry Park was another winter playground, north of town, where parents brought their children there to play, ski and sled amid the deep snow of the park. Soon, others had ideas and visions of a future for Steamboat Springs and its glorious snow. It began with a young man who earned medals and prestige in a new winter sport emerging in Europe. Carl Howelsen immigrated to America in 1904. A native of Norway, Howelsen grew up with skiing as a necessity, much like the natives of Steamboat. By the turn of the century, skiing as a sport was indeed beginning to take hold in the mountain areas of Europe. By the time Howelsen came to America, he had emerged as one of Europe's most accomplished skiers, winning the gold medal at Holmenkollen, as well as the cross-country competition the Nordic Combination and the Crown Prince Silver Cup.

In 1913, Howelsen, who had learned of the fabulous snow conditions and the cross-country skiing enthusiasts of Routt County, arrived in Steamboat Springs. It just so happened that Howelsen, in search of employment, was hired by a local architect, A.E. Gumprecht, as a mason for his latest building project.[60] That building project was the new St. Paul's Episcopal Church.

The first Episcopal church, St. Paul's Protestant Episcopal Church, conducted its first services in a building located on Lincoln Avenue in 1889. Years later, when the building was purchased and became the Welcome Hotel, the congregation held services in a room at the old courthouse.[61] After years of fundraising, the Episcopalian congregation purchased a corner lot at Ninth and Oak Streets to erect a permanent house of worship. Designed and built by A.E. Gumprecht, the church was constructed of local

St. Paul's Episcopal Church in Steamboat Springs. The author and her godson were baptized here in 1984. *Courtesy of St. Paul's Episcopal Church.*

ashlar sandstone, and the exterior was enhanced with several stained-glass windows. The interior offered an open atmosphere with the tall ceiling beams, contrasting with the simple whitewashed walls. The sanctuary, with its oak pews, also featured a hand-carved golden oak altar. Archdeacon E.W. Sibbald, along with Bishop Benjamin Brewster, traveled to Steamboat Springs to conduct the dedication ceremonies.[62]

In July 1925, the congregation purchased a "very handsome" bungalow on Seventh Street to be used as a vicarage.

The year 1911 was a banner year for the extreme northwestern corner of the state. The Denver and Rio Grande Railroad finally arrived in the town of Craig, freeing the area from near isolation. That same year, a portion of the extreme western edge of Routt County became Moffat County, named for railroad builder David H. Moffat, extending westward to the Utah state line.

In 1889, the town of Craig was established by, and named for, Alexander C. Craig and William Bayard Craig, who were not related. Craig had served the ranching and farming community for years by the time it became the county seat in 1911.

Under the leadership of Reverend William Bayard Craig, the first church built in the town of Craig was the First Christian Church. Located on the northeast end of Yampa Street, the town's main thoroughfare, construction of the Carpenter Gothic structure began in 1893. The small A-frame church included a shake-shingle roof, as well as a square two-story bell tower capped with a steepled crowned roof. Completed in the late summer of 1894, the dedication service was held on Sunday, November 18, 1894. Four years later, in September 1898, the congregation finally received a bell, which was ceremoniously installed in the church's bell tower. Tragedy struck on February 14, 1901, when the church caught fire and burned to the ground. The congregation took action, and within a year, the Christian Church was rebuilt at the same location. The original Carpenter Gothic architectural style was again employed, including the same A-frame construction, culminating in a steeply pitched gabled roof. Above the southwest corner double-door entrance was an octagonal bell tower. The 1898 bell, the only thing to survive the fire, was again installed in the new bell tower. Over the years, as additions were made to accommodate the needs of the Craig community, the new Christian Church became fondly known throughout the town as the "Center of Craig."[63] (Colorado State Register, 12/9/1992, 5MF.3377.)

In 1901, the Congregational Church was built in Craig. *Courtesy of Museum of Northwest Colorado.*

In 1901, the Congregational Church was built on the corner of Main and Tucker Streets. The Carpenter Gothic building included rectangular windows with detailed wooden frames. The bell tower, built at the corner, featured an open area below the steeple where the bell was proudly hung. Two years later, a two-story clapboard parsonage was built next to the church. For the next fifty years, the Congregational Church served the community of Craig from this location.

In 1958, the Congregational Church was moved to a site on Green Street, next to where a new "modern" church building had been built. Today, the 1901 Congregational Church, along with the newer church building, serve the Episcopal and Methodist community of Craig.

CHAPTER 3

The Arkansas River Valley

When he had finished praying, Jesus and his disciples crossed the valley and on the other side there was a garden and the disciples went into it.
—John 18:1

Bent County, created in 1874, was named for the famed frontier fort established in 1833 by William and Charles Bent.[64] Located strategically along the banks of the Arkansas River, Bent's Fort became the popular stopping point along the Santa Fe Trail for both west- and eastbound travelers. In the spring of 1867, heavy rainfall caused rivers and streams to overflow their banks. By June, the rushing Arkansas River had caused flooding all along the Arkansas Valley. On the distant southeastern plains, the ravaging flood destroyed Fort Wise, more commonly known as the first Fort Lyon. The United States Army relocated the fort two miles upstream, about one mile below the mouth of the Arkansas and Purgatory Rivers. On June 9, 1867, the new Fort Lyon military post was established.[65] Among the various military buildings—including officers' quarters, barracks for enlisted men, a kitchen and mess hall and a one-room facility for the fort's doctor—a chapel was also constructed. Built of native stone, it was a small single-story structure with only two rooms. Nevertheless, the chapel provided a place for those so inclined to worship. The chapel also was used for funerals of the fallen, many of whom were laid to rest in thc fort's cemetery.[66] It was also in this historic chapel that Christopher Houston "Kit" Carson died.

In late January 1868, General Carson was among many Colorado dignitaries called to Washington, D.C., by the War Department for a conference on how best to prevent Indian uprisings. Despite his declining health, Carson agreed to accompany Colorado governor Alexander C. Hunt and headed the Ute delegation of chiefs and dignitaries, including his friend Chief Ouray, for a peace council with President Andrew Johnson and members of both the U.S. Senate and House of Representatives.

On the return trip, Carson became very ill but managed to make it to his home at Boggsville. Two days later, on April 13, 1868, Carson's wife, Josefa, gave birth to the couple's seventh child. While the baby girl was healthy, Josefa

Christopher "Kit" Carson died on May 23, 1868, at Fort Lyon. *Courtesy of Denver Public Library.*

was quite weak and remained in bed for days. As Carson sat by his wife's side, confident Josefa would be fine, he wrote a letter to a friend, relaying such optimism: "I arrived home on the 11th inst. and found my family well. I was very sick but since my arrival home, I have improved some & hope it will continue."[67] Sadly, a few days later, April 27, 1868, Josefa died. Carson finally gave the baby girl a name, Josefita, in honor of her mother and his beloved wife.

Perhaps due to his grief, Carson's health rapidly deteriorated. On May 14, 1868, Thomas Boggs hitched his wagon and drove the ailing Carson to Fort Lyon. There, Dr. Henry R. Tilton thoroughly examined Carson. Dr. Tilton later described the situation: "His [Carson] disease, aneurysm of the aorta, had progressed rapidly; and the tumor pressing on the pneumo-gastric nerves and trachea caused frequent spasms of the bronchial tubes which were exceedingly distressing."[68]

Fearing that Carson would not live much longer, Dr. Tilton moved the Civil War general to the chapel for his patient's comfort as well as privacy. For the next two weeks, Dr. Tilton tended to his only patient day and night, doing what he could to ease Carson's pain. The two became fast friends. Carson's only visitors were his two oldest sons and his longtime friend Thomas Boggs, who agreed to raise the Carson children. At 4:25 p.m. on May 23, 1868,

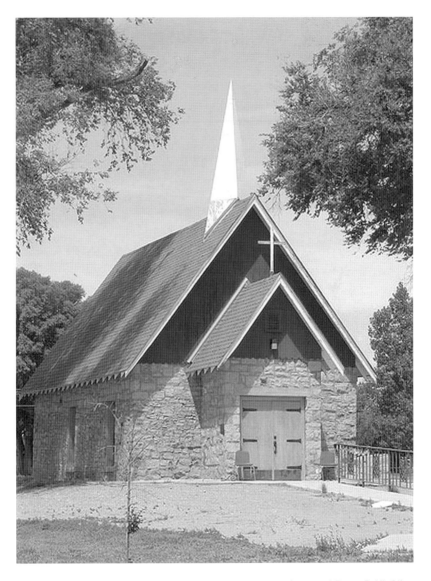

Christopher "Kit" Carson died in this chapel at Fort Lyon. *Courtesy of Denver Public Library.*

Carson began coughing, and blood spurted from his mouth. "I supported his forehead on my hand while death speedily closed the scene," wrote Dr. Tilton.[69] Carson's last words in Spanish were, "*Adios compadre.*"

With the passing of General Christopher Houston "Kit" Carson, the commander of Fort Lyon ordered the American flag flying high over Fort

Lyon lowered to half-mast. Dr. Henry Tilton spent that evening secluded in the chapel, preparing his friend's body for burial. The following day, after a brief ceremony that included rifle volleys and the playing of taps, Fort Lyon soldiers led a procession to Boggsville, carrying the casket of General Christopher Carson. Upon arrival at Boggsville that solemn day, the Fort Lyon soldiers carried the casket to the grave next to his beloved wife, Josefa.[70]

Following the end of the Indian wars, Fort Lyon was decommissioned in 1887. Then, in 1906, the fort was recommissioned as a United States naval medical facility to treat tubercular patients. While rows of new brick buildings were built, a few of the original structures were torn down. One of the twelve original buildings that remained was the chapel. In honor of General Christopher Houston "Kit" Carson, the chapel was later renamed the Kit Carson Memorial Chapel. (Colorado State Register, 5BN.420.)

In 1886, the small town of Las Animas became the seat of Bent County. In 1919, the Las Animas Christian Church was built in Classical Revival style. Located at 502 Locust Street, the church is perhaps the finest example of the "Akron Plan." Incorporated into the interior design of churches in the early 1900s, the Akron Plan provided dual purposes of rooms in smaller churches. Folding sliding doors were installed in the back of the sanctuary to create Sunday school rooms. Conversely, the doors would remain open providing additional room for larger church functions. (Colorado State Register, 5/14/1997, 5BN.449.)

One of the original counties of Colorado Territory, Las Animas County is also the largest county in the state. The town of Trinidad became the county seat and remains so today. In 1865, Trinidad pioneer Don Felipe Baca and his wife, Dolores, were instrumental in building one of the first churches in the town. Constructed of adobe, the small house of worship was named for the couple's daughter, Trinity.

In 1885, parishioners of the Holy Trinity Catholic Church hired architect Charles Innes to build a new house of worship. Father Charles Pinto replaced the small adobe chapel that had served the community for several years with a Romanesque Revival building. Built of local sandstone, the rounded windows and entryway were trimmed in Georgian massing.

Inside, the chapel was simply stunning. The sixty-foot-tall, barrel-vaulted ceiling lent an open air atmosphere, along with polished wood-paneled walls and windows with glistening stained glass. Dedication ceremonies were conducted by Father Charles Pinto, the congregation's first Jesuit pastor. Until the year 1919, the Holy Trinity Catholic Church served as the main ministry

Trinidad's Holy Trinity Catholic Church was built in 1888. *Courtesy of Denver Public Library.*

Interior of the Holy Trinity Catholic Church in Trinidad. *Courtesy of Denver Public Library.*

for more than sixty missions scattered throughout the county. (Colorado State Register, 5LA.4483.)

In 1889, C.W. Bulger and Isaac H. Rapp erected the city's first synagogue. Located at the southwest corner of Maple and Third Streets, the square two-story building, built on an upslope, was quite impressive. Temple Aaron was built of red brick and flanked at the front by two corner towers. Above the stoned arched entrance was a central rose window. The windows and entryways were all trimmed in natural white sandstone. Rising from the roof was an octagonal-topped tower with an onion-shaped dome.

Rabbi F. Freudenthal was the first leader and remained in that position for twenty-seven years. In 1989, the congregation celebrated the 100th anniversary of Temple Aaron. It was also in 1989 that the historic structure was donated by the congregation to the Colorado Historical Society to serve as a museum if and when the synagogue was no longer useful.[71] To date, Temple Aaron remains an important house of worship and an equally important historic Trinidad landmark. Temple Aaron is considered to be the oldest synagogue not only in Colorado but also in the Rocky Mountain West. (Colorado State Register, 5LA.4839.)

Trinidad's First Baptist Church was built in 1890. Late Victorian architectural features were implemented in the native sandstone structure. Designed and built by the Trinidad architectural firm of Charles W. Bugler and Isaac Hamilton Rapp, it is considered its finest work of the several Trinidad buildings it constructed. (5LA.8697.)

Reverend Theodore Hawley designed and built the First Presbyterian Church in 1902. Hawley, who received his architecture degree from Illinois's Carthage College, used elements of Gothic Revival in constructing the brick church. The square building, at the corner of Commercial and Elm Streets, included several arched windows but, curiously, no bell tower. (5LA.4220.)

In 1842, trappers and traders—including James P. Beckwourth, Richens L. "Uncle Dick" Wootton and Joseph Doyle—built an adobe trading post near the confluence of the Arkansas River and Fountain Creek. The men named it El Pueblo, meaning "village" in Spanish. However, in 1854, the fort was attacked on Christmas Day by a band of Ute Indians. Although the fort was never rebuilt, settlement eventually did come to the area. Fred A. Hale built Pueblo's First Congregational Church in 1889. When it was completed, the citizens of Pueblo were very pleased, including the *Colorado Chieftain*, which described the new church in detail in the October 3, 1889 issue of the paper: "The church is a regular little gem in church architecture, complete and perfect in every respect. The walls are built of pink stone, cut to represent the natural fracture of the rock, and consequently do not present any of the parallel lines and right angles which are usually seen in cut stonework."

The First Congregational Church is listed in the National Register. (2/8/1985, 5PE.4209.)

Reverend Sheldon Jackson, the devoted Presbyterian missionary, arrived in Pueblo some twenty years after he founded his first church in Fairplay. In 1890, Reverend Jackson built the First Presbyterian Church of Pueblo, constructed on the southeast corner of Court and Tenth Streets. The Richardsonian Romanesque building was built of natural red sandstone. Dark-red mortar created accented detail to the natural stone trimming. The

First Presbyterian Church in Pueblo. *Courtesy of Denver Public Library.*

traditional arched windows contained Tiffany stained glass, a gift to the church from John A. and Margaret H. Thatcher. (Colorado State Register, 5PE.4288.)

In 1891, Pueblo's African American community built a church of brick on the southwest corner of Eighth Street. The Gothic-style church featured arched windows of leaded glass. The Eighth Street Baptist Church became a cultural and social as well as religious center. (Colorado State Register, 5PE.4289.)

In 1907, Pueblo's St. John's Greek Orthodox Church was erected on Spruce Street. Following the Classical Revival style, the house of worship also included unusual aspects of the style. The 2002 Historic Preservation assessment described the exterior: "The building exhibits the distinctive characteristics of the style in its full-width pedimented portico supported by large Ionic columns. The semi-circular transom and round-arched window openings with Queen Anne–inspired glazing result in an unusual expression of the style." St. John's Greek Orthodox Church is listed in the National Register. (2/28/2002, 5PE.4219.)

The Sacred Heart Church was built in 1912 on the southwest corner of Grand Avenue and Eleventh Street. Denver architect Montana S. Fallis and Robert Willison designed the French Gothic Revival building. Constructed of speckled tan brick and trimmed with terra cotta, the structure included stained-glass windows created by the Emil Frei Studio in St. Louis, Missouri. The matching corner octagon spire was flanked by two square towers. Above the triple arched entrance a large rose window was installed, which was also handcrafted in St. Louis, Missouri.

In 1942, Pueblo became the seat of the Catholic Diocese of Southern Colorado. At the same time, Sacred Heart Church was expanded, renovated and renamed Sacred Heart Cathedral. (National Register, 2/21/1989, 5PE.1125.)

In 1913, Frank E. Wetherell, of the Iowa architectural firm of Wetherell & Gage, arrived in Pueblo to design and build the Church of the Ascension. Constructed of brick and trimmed in sandstone, Wetherell used many elements of the Tudor Revival style. In 1926, a rectory built of stucco and brick was constructed on the west side of the church. A parish hall was added in 1941. (Colorado State Register, 3/13/2002, 5PE.4175.)

Another of the original counties formed following Colorado's Territorial status in 1861, El Paso County claims ranch land, foothills and mountains, including Pikes Peak. In 1871, General William Jackson Palmer created the town of Colorado Springs, which became the county seat.

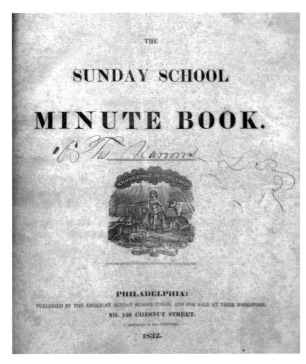

Left: A children's Sunday school program. *Courtesy of Library of Congress*.

Below: The First Congregational Church in Colorado Springs was built in 1889. *Courtesy of Denver Public Library*.

In 1874, a group of the First Congregationalists formed in Colorado Springs. This group was closely associated with the early history and development of Colorado College. In 1889, two architect firms, Henry Rutgers Marshall of New York and Robert S. Roeschlaub of Denver, teamed together to design and build the First Congregational Church. Located at the northwest corner of St. Vrain and Tejon Streets, the church was constructed of natural stone. A tall square tower was the dominant feature of this house of worship. While elements of Classical Greek were incorporated in the style, it was the finest example of Richardsonian Romanesque architecture in Colorado Springs. Perhaps the most striking element of the two styles were the contrasting roofs. The church's roof was rather plain with broad planes, while the square tower was crowned with a pyramid roof. Immense stone columns supported the balcony over the front porch. (National Register, 10/31/2002, 5EP.631.)

In 1890, the congregation of the First Church of Colorado City purchased a corner lot on South Twenty-Fourth Street. By this time, the original town of Colorado City had become a western suburb of Colorado Springs. Walter F. Douglas, a prominent local architect, built the church in the Late Victorian style. Architectural elements included a square corner tower, a second-story balcony and a gabled roof. A local tale involves one of the pastors, Reverend Lamont. One day in 1907, following a fire that destroyed several saloons along Colorado Avenue, the good reverend was publicly extolling his pleasure at their destruction whereupon a group of firemen turned their hoses on him.[72]

In 1917, the church building was purchased by the Baptist congregation and renamed the Bethany Baptist Church. In 1995, the historic church was placed in the Colorado State Register of Historic Properties. It was also during this time that a grant was awarded that allowed for restoration. Following the restoration, the building became the location for the Old Colorado City History Center. The building is the last intact example of Colorado City's early churches. (Colorado State Register, 6/14/1995, 5EP.597.)

In Colorado Springs, the First Baptist Church was built at the southeast corner of Kiowa and Weber Streets in 1891. The Brooklyn, New York architectural firm of L.B. Valk and Son designed the Neo-Romanesque church, built of pressed brick. The brick walls were accented with red sandstone and contained arched windows. The Omaha Art Stained Glass Company created the glass with naturalistic flora. The roof was enhanced with gabled dormers. A square tower rose above the roof line with matching red sandstone accents. (Colorado State Register, 5EP.231.)

Spencer and Julie Penrose built Pauline Chapel in honor of their granddaughter in 1919. Today, the chapel along with the Pauline Memorial Catholic School, next to the Pauline Chapel, are in the National Register of Historic Places. *Courtesy of Denver Public Library.*

In 1891, a groundbreaking ceremony marked the beginning of the construction of the St. Mary's Catholic Cathedral at 26 West Kiowa Street. It would be a ten-year endeavor. When completed in 1902, the Gothic Revival church included two bell towers constructed of pressed red brick, as was the church itself. Natural limestone was used in the framing of the windows, including the large rose window at the front of the church. Above this window, a statue of St. Mary was placed in a niche in the brick wall. (National Register, 6/3/1982, 5EP.208.)

Spencer and Julie Penrose, perhaps Colorado Springs' wealthiest couple, were also involved in many charitable organizations in the city. In particular, Julie, a devout Catholic, gave both her time and money to the church. Three years after the Penrose couple purchased the Broadmoor Hotel, Julie Penrose was instrumental in organizing a large Colorado Springs parade. It was the celebration of the return of the American soldiers following the end of World War I. The parade, held on April 26, 1919, was a gala affair and featured Julie's four-year-old granddaughter, the Baroness Pauline de Ways Ruart, dressed in a Belgian costume. Shortly after the parade, young Pauline became gravely ill. Julie Penrose prayed and relied on her faith to see her precious granddaughter through the illness. When Pauline recovered, Julie prevailed on her husband to build the Pauline Chapel in honor of their granddaughter, who would later become the Baroness Pauline Francois de Longchamps.[73]

Spencer Penrose hired the prominent local architectural firm of Thomas McLaren and T.E. Hetherington to design and construct the chapel in a grove of pine trees behind his Broadmoor Hotel. McLaren built a small Spanish Baroque chapel. At the entrance to Pauline Chapel stood a statue of St. Paul. Julie Penrose remained committed to the chapel, collecting religious art that would grace the chapel. Later, Julie Penrose was instrumental in the building of the Pauline Memorial Catholic School, next to the Pauline Chapel. When the religious property was placed in the National Register of Historic Properties in 2001, the 1925 Mission-inspired rectory and garage were included. (National Register, 2/26/2001, 5EP.3182.)

In 1954, under President Dwight D. Eisenhower, Colorado Springs became the awarded site for America's first United States Air Force Academy. Located at the base of the foothills north of the city, the academy grounds covered more than eighteen thousand acres. Nestled up next to those foothills, almost in the center of the academy's oblong acreage, the Academy Chapel was built in 1963. The most noticeable feature of the chapel were the seventeen spires. The aluminum-clad stained-glass panels are set in frames consisting of tetrahedral steel piping. Due to the Modernist interpretation of Gothic architecture, the Academy Chapel, at a cost of $3 million, is today Colorado's most famous church.

Just a few short miles up the canyon from Colorado Springs are the natural mineral springs for which Colorado Springs is named. Dr. William Bell established a health resort community in the area in 1871 that he called Manitou Springs.

Local Congregationalists held Sunday religious services in a tent for more than two years. In 1880, the Congregationalists set about building a church. The small wooden structure was built at the edge of Fountain Creek. Not long after completion, the creek flooded, severely damaging the structure. Somehow, the church was moved to the opposite side of Fountain Creek. Today, the First Congregational Church in Manitou Springs is Colorado's oldest Congregational church. (National Register, 10/16/1979, 5EP.185.)

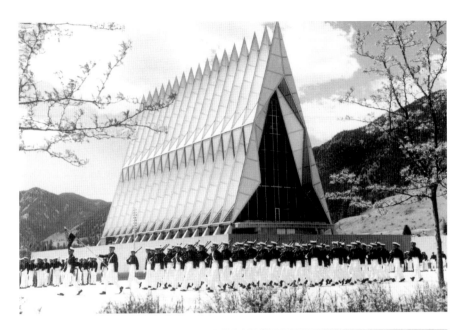

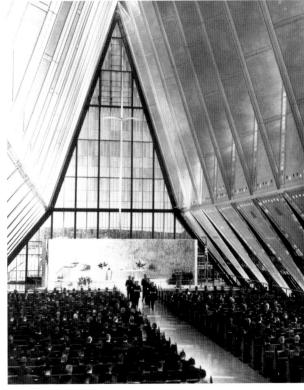

Above: The United States Air Force Academy Chapel was built in 1963. *Courtesy of Denver Public Library.*

Right: The interior of the United States Air Force Academy Chapel is nothing short of spectacular. *Courtesy of Denver Public Library.*

In 1904, Angus Gillis was commissioned to design and build St. Andrew's Episcopal Church. The new building replaced the outgrown church just down the block. The Queen Anne–style church, with Gothic overtones, was constructed of native red sandstone. The one-and-a-half-story building included a slate roof imported from England. A tall bell tower completed the exterior of the building. Inside, stained-glass windows were prevalent throughout, with stamped frames that read, "E. Frampton, 110 Buckingham Palace Rd., London, England." (National Register, 5EP.675.)

A few miles west of Manitou Springs, along the winding Ute Pass Trail, the town of Cascade was established. In 1930, the prominent Frank Cusak family commissioned Colorado Springs architect Charles E. Thomas to build a Catholic chapel on their property. Thomas spent the next year building Holy Rosary Chapel. The Romanesque Revival–style church was constructed of native red rock. The arched windows and double-door entrance reflected elements of the Mission style. A wide, curved path of red rock led to a stairway constructed of long red rock slabs, leading to the chapel entrance. Inside, the red rock walls offered a rustic setting to the mountain chapel. Another winding red rock stairway led to the basement area. There, a stone grotto had been designed, modeled after the Shrine of Our Lady of Lourdes in France.[74] Soft lighting lent to the quiet atmosphere for a place of devotion.

When the chapel was completed in 1931, Charles E. Thomas considered the small building in the mountains as "one of his most outstanding works."[75] The first mass was conducted by Archbishop John Urban Vehr. Years later, the Frank Cusak family donated Holy Rose Chapel to the Colorado Catholic diocese. The historic chapel then served as the Parish of Sacred Heart in Colorado Springs. (Colorado State Register, 12/13/1995, 5EP.2210.)

Elbert County, created in 1874, was named for then Territorial Governor Samuel Hitt Elbert, the son-in-law of Territorial Governor John Evans. The region has always been known for its farming and ranching.

In 1889, Jacob Frick, one of the county's earliest settlers, donated land in the town of Elbert, the county seat, for the Presbyterian church. Reverend S.R. Shull, who had often traveled from Colorado Springs to offer his services, did so again to help raise the needed funds for building materials. When $1,500 had been raised, members of the Presbyterian congregation worked together to construct the house of worship. One such member, Justice of the Peace Taylor Green, lent his carpenter skills to build the St. Mark's Presbyterian Church on Main Street. The Carpenter Gothic–style church, with a wooden foundation, was erected on a hillside. A long wooden staircase was built leading to the church entrance from Main Street. The entrance was dominated by a tall square bell tower capped with a four-sided cupola. The high gabled roof supported a brick chimney. Inside, the simple décor was enhanced by the handmade pews provided by Taylor Green. Over the years, additions have been made to the structure.

On Memorial Day 1935, heavy rains caused Kiowa Creek to flood, destroying more than sixty buildings in Elbert. Fortunately, because the church was built on a hill, St. Mark's Presbyterian Church was spared. The church became the care center for the less fortunate citizens, as well as distributing food and clothing to those in need. In 1940, a bell was donated and originally mounted atop the church. However, with each ringing of the bell, the entire building shook. Eventually, a bell tower was erected, and the bell was placed in the belfry. St. Mark's Presbyterian Church was the first Protestant church to be organized and built in Elbert County. (National Register, 9/18/1980, 5EL.138.)

In 1859, early pioneers Newton S. Grout and brothers Guy and Upton Smith settled on the banks of upper West Plum Creek in Douglas County. The area was well known by the Ute Indians because of the junction of several small creeks, including Indian Creek, Plum Creek and both East

St. Philip-in-the-Field Church, in Douglas County, was built in 1870. *Author's collection.*

St. Mark's Presbyterian Church is located on Main Street in Elbert. *Author's collection.*

and West Plum Creeks. John Craig capitalized on the creek junction by establishing the first Territorial Road, which ran along Plum Creek, south to Colorado City or north to Denver. In 1869, Grout, the Smith brothers and others established the town of Plum, named for the abundance of plum trees. This was the beginning of the agricultural community later renamed Sedalia.

The following year, David T. Wolf deeded three acres of his land for the community cemetery. In his deed, Wolf stipulated that the graveyard should be free to all settlers.[76] In February 1870, organizers of the Bear Canon Methodist Church formed the first such congregation in Douglas County. The foundation for the church was laid very near the center of the Bear Canon Cemetery. Built by Newton S. Grout, the white clapboard building resembled the typical Carpenter Gothic style yet also reflected the Gothic Revival style with its pitched roof and arched windows. When completed, Grout named the new church St. Philip-in-the-Field Church, after his native New England home's style of churches. During Colorado's centennial anniversary celebration in 1976, Pastor Robert Hier wrote:

> *St. Philip-in-the-Field Church and Bear Canon Cemetery represent in the relatively new section of our country a sense of continuity with the past and hope for the future without which, human beings would not be human. St. Philip is an emblem of the best of old life and new. It is a link to the past, the present and the future—to make manifest the usually forgotten bonds between our ancestors and ourselves.[77]*

The St. Philip-in-the-Field Church and Bear Canon Cemetery are listed as historic properties under 5DA.212, Bear Canon Agricultural District, as well as the National Register. (4/11/1973, 5DA.217.)

The town of Castle Rock, established in 1871, began as a farming community. In 1888, the Catholic community of Castle Rock raised the necessary funds to build their own house of worship. Land was purchased on the corner of Third and Jerry Streets. Catholic parishioner John Baptiste Ehmanon offered his stonemason expertise to build the new church. Ehmanon took advantage of the local rhyolite stone quarries abundant in the Castle Rock area. The natural rough-faced rhyolite stone dominated the exterior of the building. A rose window graced the edifice of the new St. Francis of Assisi Catholic Church. When completed, the Catholic house of worship was the first church built in Castle Rock.

In 1966, the parish moved to a larger facility. The former church was purchased in 1975. Restored and remodeled by the owners, the building became a restaurant. Known as the Old Stone Church Restaurant, the owners have retained the historical charm of the building. (Colorado State Register, 5DA.210.)

One of the original counties formed in 1861, Lake County was known for its gold strikes near the headwaters of the Arkansas River. Oro City, a gold mining camp, served as the first county seat. In 1877, following the rich silver strikes on Fryer Hill, a new mining camp, Leadville, became the county seat. Today, the town of Leadville is one of Colorado's few historic towns listed as a National Historic Landmark District.

St. George's Episcopal Church in Leadville is most unusual for a mountain mining town. Despite the fire dangers typical of such communities, this house of worship was built of wood. In 1880, W.P. Westworth began construction of the church at the northwest corner of Fourth and Pine Streets. The Gothic Revival style is evident throughout the structure. The small frame building included a bell tower above the entrance, with a central, open belfry. The bell was a gift to the Episcopal congregation from Leadville's "Silver King," Horace A.W. Tabor. The Gothic-style structure was capped with a steep pitched roof, completed with an attractive truss.[78] Fine examples of the Gothic style of intricate timbering include the side wings, with wooden buttresses, extending from the roof. Another feature were the Gothic lancets that framed the stained-glass windows. Over the A-frame entrance, a rose window, framed within a wooden arch, contained four smaller round stained-glass windows. The interior carried the same Gothic architecture, including a tracker organ manufactured by the Ryder Company in Boston, Massachusetts. This organ was hauled by wagon in pieces over the two-mile-high Mosquito Pass. (5LK.)

Another church erected in the "Cloud City" was the Annunciation Catholic Church. It was the vision of Father Henry Robinson ever since his arrival in Leadville. Robinson, a native of Salem, Illinois, was ordained in Denver on January 21, 1872. After establishing Catholic parishes in mountain mining camps such as Alma and Fairplay, Father Robinson arrived in the bustling mining town of Leadville in February 1878. Years later, Father Robinson recalled his first observation upon his arrival: "There was one church. Some of the citizens from whom I made inquiry doubted the existence of a church."[79]

For the next few months, Father Robinson held Catholic services in the homes of Catholic families. By the summer, Leadville's first Catholic church, Sacred Heart, had been built at the corner of Third and Spruce Streets. Before the end of the summer, it had become clear that the one-room wooden structure was too small to hold Leadville's Catholic parishioners.

In the fall of 1878, a group of the Sisters of Charity arrived from Leavenworth, Kansas. After a meeting with the Sisters, Father Robinson asked them to stay in Leadville and help with charitable causes. In early January 1879, three of the Sisters—Crescentia Fischer, Bernard Mary

Pendergast and Francis Xavier—paid a visit to Father Robinson at his home. The Sisters were shocked at Robinson's weak condition, as he was "pale and emaciated, wrapped in a buffalo robe, and sitting by the side of a drum-stove which had one very long stick of wood in it, the door partially open to accommodate it. On top of the stove sat a small bucket of water."[80]

While the Sisters nursed Father Robinson back to health from a bout of pneumonia, the Sisters realized the need for a hospital in Leadville. Father Robinson agreed and pledged his assistance in helping to establish a hospital. However, Father Robinson had a request of his own: he wanted the Sisters' help in soliciting charitable donations to build a new church.

The good Sisters were able to raise enough funds for the Catholic congregation to purchase the corner lot of East Seventh and Poplar Streets. Construction of the new church began immediately. Considering the high risk of fire, the Annunciation Catholic Church was built of red brick. The two-story Gothic building included many highlights of local stonemasonry. The arched windows, as well as the arched doorway, were accented with stone trimming. At the corner section of the church, a buttressed tower included an arcaded belfry topped by a metal-clad octagonal steeple. This steeple, more than one hundred feet high, became the landmark in Leadville architecture.[81] Despite the ongoing construction of the interior of the church, the first mass was held on New Year's Day 1880. Among the many services, funerals and weddings conducted in the church over the years was the September 1, 1886 wedding of James J. Brown and Margaret Tobin. Mrs. Margaret Tobin Brown would later survive the sinking of the *Titanic* in 1912, becoming forever known in history as the "Unsinkable Molly Brown." The funeral for Elizabeth "Baby Doe" Bonduel McCourt Tabor was also held here in March 1935. Today, the tall white steeple of Leadville's Annunciation Catholic Church still towers over the historic silver mining town. (5LK.)

In 1896, Bishop Nicholas Matz sent Father John Perse to Leadville to establish a second Catholic parish to serve the large Slovenian immigrant population. On the afternoon of December 17, 1899, a procession of church members left the Annunciation Catholic Church and walked down Harrison Avenue to the site of the new St. Joseph's Catholic Church. Father Perse conducted the cornerstone-laying ceremony, and the Leadville Miners Band provided the music. Construction of the Carpenter Gothic church was completed in early 1900. Father Perse offered the first mass in early February 1900. Father John Perse served as the leader of St. Joseph's Catholic Church until 1915. At that time, Father Judnic was assigned to the parish.[82]

Tragedy struck in March 1923. Somehow the church caught on fire and burned to the ground. The congregation managed to raise $30,000 by July 1923 to rebuild its church. On August 13, 1923, Father Judnic conducted the cornerstone-laying ceremony. In less than four months, St. Joseph's Catholic Church had been rebuilt, this time of brick. However, when the congregation gathered for mass on Christmas Eve 1923, it was standing room only. While the brick house of worship was completed, the interior was entirely another matter—with no pews installed, the members stood through the mass on that holy day of worship. (5LK.)

The town of Salida was established in 1880, following the arrival of the Denver and Rio Grande Railroad. Five years later, local citizens came together to build the Church of the Ascension. The location of the new church, on E Street, replaced a previous church building. The simple wood-frame structure featured elements of the traditional Carpenter Gothic style, including arched windows and a gabled roof. The only remaining religious structure built during the early years of Salida, the historical Church of the Ascension remains a vital part of the community today. In 1952, an original stained-glass window from the Denver and Rio Grande Hospital was installed on the west side of the church. (Colorado State Register 6/14/2000 5CF.344.)

CHAPTER 4

The Rio Grande River Valley

Therefore I will make a place for planting vineyards.
The valley will be laid with foundations.
—Micah 1:6

Costilla County, one of the original seventeen counties included in Colorado Territory, was centered on Culebra Creek, a tributary of the mighty Rio Grande. The area had been settled as early as 1846 by farmers and ranchers. Several small communities existed; however, the only incorporated town, San Luis, became the county seat.

In 1853, Spanish missionaries established a small settlement not far from the new border between New Mexico and Colorado Territory. According to local legend, the settlers were under constant attack from the Ute Indians until San Acacio, the mission's patron saint, a Roman soldier, appeared on horseback. The ghostly image so frightened the Ute warriors that they fled, never to return. At an elevation of more than 7,700 thousand feet, Viejo San Acacio lay along Culebra Creek, where the missionaries built a chapel as a token of their gratitude to San Acacio. Three years later, a new chapel was constructed in the southwest corner of the town's plaza.[83] The adobe structure contained walls that were eighteen inches thick. A flat roof was supported by vigas, each of which was sixteen inches in circumference.

In 1910, the Viejo San Acacio Chapel was restored and renovated. A new shake-shingle pitched roof replaced the original. A wooden-frame bell tower was built, and a bronze bell was obtained. An adobe plaster

Father Joseph Projectus Machebeuf was instrumental in forming Catholic parishes throughout Colorado. *Courtesy of Denver Public Library.*

Viejo San Acacio Chapel in Costilla County is one of the oldest churches in Colorado. *Courtesy of Kenneth Jessen.*

was applied to the exterior and interior walls. Vertical double-hung windows replaced the original adobe framed windows. Inside the chapel, varnished wooden posts and beams supported the new roof and newly installed choir loft.

A second renovation occurred in 1990. When the original floor was removed, making way for a new polished wooden floor, several graves were discovered just a few feet below. In an effort not to disturb the remains, carpenters raised the floor of the altar. Today, the adobe Viejo San Acacio Chapel sits pristine alongside the courtyard and next to the century-old cemetery.[84] (Colorado State Register, 5CT.21.)

San Luis is the oldest continuously inhabited town in the state. As such, the entire community, including the town plaza, known as the Plaza de San Luis de Culebra, is now in the register of Colorado's Historic Districts.

In 1854, a small chapel was built at the northern end of the town plaza. In 1886, a French missionary priest, Reverend Jean-Baptiste Pitival, built the Sangre de Cristo Catholic Church near the plaza. Constructed of adobe, it included Gothic elements such as arched windows and doors. The steep gable roof supported a bell tower over the entrance to the church. Over the next thirty years, the Sangre de Cristo Catholic Church remained largely unchanged, save for an exterior upgrade in 1900. That year, a tan cement stucco was applied to the adobe.

Twenty years later, in 1920, a chapel was erected behind the church that included pews and an altar handmade with mail-order materials.[85]

The Conejos Land Grant was one of many Mexican land grants that were offered along the Mexican border with the United States. Created by the Mexican government in 1830, the idea was to offer the land grants to loyal Mexican citizens in an effort to fortify the northern Mexico border with the United States in the event of war. In 1833, a group of settlers, led by Seledon Valdez, was awarded the Conejos Land Grant. The land encompassed 1,600 square miles, bounded by the San Juan Mountain range to the west and the Rio Grande to the east, as well as from Mount San Antonio, the northern Mexico landmark, to the La Garita Mountain range of the American side of the border. This was the San Luis Valley, which became the first permanent settlement in what would become the state of Colorado. It was a fertile area, perfect for farming and ranching. Over the next few decades, Seledon Valdez, his friends and family built their homes in the valley and raised their families.

On August 18, 1846, the short-lived Mexican-American War ended when General Stephen Watts Kearny and his army triumphantly entered the northern Mexico governing town of Santa Fe and raised the American flag without firing a shot. Following the Mexican surrender, negotiations between officials of the two nations to establish the boundary between the two countries determined to move it to the Rio Grande in south Texas.

In 1854, the town of Conejos was established in the southern area of Colorado. According to local historian Patricia Sanchez Rau, "The first settlers into the area were from New Mexico, primarily from Abiquiu, San Juan de los Caballeros, and Santa Cruz. They also established schools in the area and had a large number of Hispanic converts. As more and more people arrived, mission churches were set up."[86]

In an effort to reestablish civil control following the war, as well as "Americanize" the Mexican Catholic parishes, Bishop Jean B. Lamy was named the vicar apostolic of the southwestern area, including southern Colorado. Bishop Lamy encouraged Catholic missionaries to lead settlers into the southern Colorado area to accomplish this act.

According to ancient folklore, a group of Mexican settlers, led by Nuestra Señora de Guadalupe, left the Rio Grande and headed west toward the Conejos River. This group of settlers was said to be guided northwest to the Conejos River by the angel of Guadalupe in 1854. Reaching the banks of the river, their livestock refused to move farther. After hours of pushing and pulling and other various negotiations with the animals, it was discovered that the treasured statue of Our Lady of Guadalupe had fallen from the cargo that one of the animals was carrying. Taken as a sign from God above, the colonists decried their good fortune and started their heaven-sent settlement on that very spot.

Our Lady of Guadalupe Roman Catholic Church was the dream of Colorado pioneer Father Joseph Projectus Machebeuf, a frail missionary who worked closely with Bishop Lamy. An adobe structure, sixteen by thirty feet, took shape, typical of early southwestern architecture such as Bent's Fort. Dried red clay bricks supported the foundation, while crossbeams supported the roof. When completed, Our Lady of Guadalupe parish became the first sanctioned Roman Catholic church in what would become the state of Colorado. Originally, the adobe church at Conejos was a mission church for priests from the three New Mexican parishes. However, under the direction of Father José Vicente Montaño, the congregation quickly grew in numbers, not surprising for the close-knit community.

In 1857, Father Machebeuf was able to acquire an adjoining lot between the church and the community plaza. Father Machebeuf, by rite of holy consecration, dedicated and gave the land over for the first Roman Catholic church in Conejos. Following the traditional New Mexican building technique, an enlarged church was built around the old one, removing the need for a completely new structure, saving costs and eliminating the disruption of religious services. Father Machebeuf returned to Conejos in 1858, at which time he said his first mass at the enlarged Our Lady of Guadalupe Catholic Church.

Father Machebeuf, who never doubted his faith, believed that this first foundation for Catholicism in Colorado would bring more missionaries and parishes to the region. Father Machebeuf and Father Gabriel Ussel spent a considerable amount of time traveling throughout the San Luis Valley spreading the word of Catholicism. Father Ussel later wrote of this period in his life: "Before dawn, by the light of pinion wood fires, priests and villagers met for the morning chanted Mass, the procession, and that little world of people came from everywhere to participate in the religious festivities, and the usual innocent amusement of a happy people. The panorama of dress, foot races, horse races, all in the open air enlivened by the musicians' band."[87]

Famed western novelist Willa Cather, author of *Death Comes for the Archbishop*, based that work's main character after Father Machebeuf. Of this time in Father Machebeuf's life, Cather wrote, "Down among the Spanish, who owned nothing but a mud house and a burro, he could always raise money. If they had anything at all, they gave."

In 1861, the United States Congress approved the Colorado Territory. President Abraham Lincoln appointed William Gilpin as territorial governor. Through his leadership and friendship with Father Machebeuf, Governor Gilpin was able to provide assistance whereby Father Machebeuf was able to offer land in Conejos County for permanent Catholic settlers.

In 1871, the Society of Jesus, known as the Jesuits, gained control of the Roman Catholic jurisdiction in the southern portion of Colorado Territory, including Conejos County. Under their leadership, Father Salvatore Persone was able to expand the Catholic fellowship to an area covering a one-hundred-mile stretch of land, with Saguache at one end and Los Piños on the other. Over the next few years, the Jesuits were successful in establishing more than a dozen Catholic parishes. Impressed with the dedication and leadership of the Jesuits, Father Machebeuf incorporated many of their ideas, which would become the cornerstone in his Catholic ministry along the front range and in mining communities. This also included the eventual formation of the Sisters of Loretto convent school in West Denver.

Our Lady of Guadalupe Catholic Church experienced a horrific tragedy in 1926, ironically on Ash Wednesday. The historic church caught fire, caused by electrical deficiencies, and received heavy damage. The repairs were made, despite some opposition from those who wanted to demolish and rebuild. The winning factor was to restore and preserve the oldest parish in Colorado on the original site.

In 1948, during a major renovation, Our Lady of Guadalupe Catholic Church received an "uplift" of sorts. Red and gray brick were used in the reconstruction of the exterior of the church. Above the arched entrance, a curvilinear parapet rose high with an arched brick recess containing a statue of Our Lady of Guadalupe. Flanked on either side were towers fifty-six feet high. The interior also received much-needed improvements. The walls were plastered in a fine shade of white, and a new pulpit was placed behind a small altar. Today, 160 years later, Our Lady of Guadalupe Catholic Church, Colorado's oldest church, remains a cornerstone of culture, steeped in history and religious tradition in the oldest area of Colorado. (Colorado State Register, 5CN.899.)

In 1880, with the arrival of the Denver and Rio Grande Railroad, the town of Antonito was established. Located just a mile south of the town of Conejos, Antonito quickly became the prominent town in the area. It was

Left: Our Lady of Guadalupe Roman Catholic Church was the dream of Colorado pioneer Father Joseph Projectus Machebeuf. It is the oldest continuously used church in the state. *Author's collection.*

Right: The interior of Our Lady of Guadalupe Roman Catholic Church is simple but eloquent. *Author's collection.*

here that the Spanish Theatine priests arrived from Spain. The following year, St. Augustine Catholic Church was built on the northwest corner of Pine Street and Eighth Avenue. The Roman Catholic parish church was built of a unique concept, combining natural stone with adobe. The Gothic stained-glass windows were neatly placed around the exterior. The heavy oak doors were hand-carved, as were the oak pews.

Under the direction of the Theatine priests, St. Augustine Catholic Church became the headquarters for the Catholic church records in the San Luis Valley: "As the Catholic missionaries expanded and grew the number of parishes throughout the valley, churches were set up and all had the records housed with the church offices of St. Augustine Catholic Church at Antonito."[88]

An unincorporated town situated along the banks of the Conejos River, Mogate was established in 1856. The town was named for the nearby triple-peaked mountain that shadowed the Conejos Canyon. In 1895, the local citizens gathered together to build the San Rafael Presbyterian Church. While built in the typical territorial adobe style of the period, the roof, which supported the bell tower, deviated from the traditional style. In this respect, the San Rafael Presbyterian Church represented the inroads the Presbyterians were able to achieve into the predominately Hispanic Catholic community of the region. Today, the San Rafael Presbyterian Church is the only Hispanic-speaking Presbyterian church in Conejos County. (Colorado State Register, 6/9/1999, 5CN.894.)

Alamosa County, named for the bustling railroad town of Alamosa, has the distinction of being the last county created in Colorado in the twentieth century. The county, carved from portions of its neighbor, Conejos County, in 1913, lay in the heart of the Rio Grande Valley. The town of Alamosa, Spanish for "cottonwood," became the county seat.

By 1881, the population of Alamosa was more than one thousand strong. New businesses were opening daily, as the railroad had opened commerce to the region. In the spring of that year, Reverend J.J. Gilcrest had arrived in the region to carry on with his mission work. Gilcrest later wrote, "In Alamosa from March to June this year. Though the town has fully 1,000 people, there was not a single sermon preached here."[89]

The following year, Reverend Alexander M. Darley built Alamosa's first church, the First Presbyterian Church. Located on the corner of San Juan and Fourth Streets, the small clapboard building included a bell tower high enough that it could be seen throughout the surrounding area. Fifteen years later, in 1896, the church was rebuilt of local sandstone. The two-story building featured three Gothic windows on all four sides. The steep gable roof included a church steeple towering above.

Located at the northeast corner of Edison Avenue and Fourth Street in Alamosa, the Sacred Heart Catholic Church was built in 1927. The large two-story brick structure, built in the Spanish Colonial Revival style, also included elements of the Spanish Mission style of architecture. The massive building stretched a quarter of a block and rose to a height of 138 feet. Designed by Denver architect Robert Willison, three tall arched doors offered entrance into the church. On each side of the Fourth Street entrance, tall, flat-topped turrets graced the building. Inside, a gorgeous vaulted ceiling, built of oak, complemented the oak flooring and oak pews. A stuccoed arcade was built in 1939, connecting the main church to the newly built rectory. In 1942, German artist Josef Steinhage painted several murals as well as a large portrait of Jesus Christ, which hangs behind the altar. The Sacred Heart Catholic Church became a parish complex that expanded to include a convent and a school. In 1953, the edifice of the church received a coat of stucco in an effort to conform to the local Hispanic influence. (Colorado State Register, 3/13/1996, 5AL.262.)

Another example of the Spanish Mission style of architecture was the construction of the St. Thomas Episcopal Church in 1926. Designed and built by the Denver architectural firm of William E. and Arthur A. Fisher, the smooth stuccoed edifice was enhanced with several round-arched windows. Low stuccoed walls were erected around the church property. An addition to the church in 1930 provided a larger sanctuary for the parishioners. (National Register, 3/4/2003, 5AL.260.)

Saguache County, established in 1867, was situated at the northern end of the spacious San Luis Valley. The eastern edge of the county gradually rises to the fourteen-thousand-foot Sangre de Cristo mountain range, while the western boundary rises to the fourteen-thousand-foot San Juan Mountains. Largely an agricultural area, the small town of Saguache became the county seat.

A happy nineteenth-century couple leave the church following their wedding. *Courtesy of Denver Public Library.*

In 1947, the citizens of Saguache came together to purchase land at the southeast corner of Gunnison Avenue and Sixth Street.[90] Librado Mondragon is credited with the construction of the St. Agnes Catholic Mission Church. Following the Pueblo Deco style, Mondragon melded unusual expressions of Art Deco with southwestern Native American designs in the stuccoed adobe structure. The Colorado State Register listing for this historic property included the following: "The church possesses the distinctive characteristics of this style as evident in its angular composition, vertical emphasis, stepped parapet, corbelled cut-outs, and geometric designs."

Raised panels, painted in a red raspberry color, framed the windows and entrance and matched the color of the roof. Above the door, a square stained-glass window was complemented with a stylized frame topped with a cross. At the rear of the church, an open bell tower was constructed, topped with a cross. (Colorado State Register, 9/10/2003, 5SH.1658.)

One of Colorado's original counties, Fremont County was named in honor of explorer John C. Frémont. Canon City, platted in 1859, became the county seat.

At the corner of Macon Avenue, the First Baptist Church was erected in 1890. Built in the architectural style of Romanesque Revival, the natural red sandstone edifice included terra-cotta trimming and several opulent windows. The large square church seemed to be a blended contrast to the tall, light-colored and vertical house of worship built ten years later. (National Register, 6/4/1988, 5EP.1145.)

Across the street, at the northeast corner of Macon Avenue and Seventh Street, the First Presbyterian Church was built in 1901. Designed and built by local architect C.C. Rittenhouse, the church was constructed of local quarried stone. Rittenhouse incorporated elements of the Queen Anne style as well as Late Victorian style in his building. The unique feature of this house of worship was the octagonal belfry, which rose above the church to the spire with nine finials pointed skyward. (National Register, 9/1/1983, 5FN.583.)

In 1924, Benedictine monks bought land two miles east of Canon City to build a boys' preparatory school. Architects Joseph Dillon and L.A. Des Jardins built Holy Cross Abbey in a medieval architectural style. Gold and brown brick were laid in an intricate pattern within a tall steel frame. The stone trimming, in French filigree designs, were quite striking in the frames of the arched windows. Elements of Gothic Revival were used in the corner tower. The interior contained a chapel, offices and a large library. (Colorado State Register, 5FN.853.)

Colorado's Wet Mountain Valley, nestled between the Wet Mountain range on the east and the Sangre de Cristo Mountains on the west, became an area of mining frenzy when silver was discovered. A year after Colorado statehood, legislation was passed creating Custer County, named for General George Armstrong Custer, who perished that year at the Battle of the Little Bighorn.

In time, mining camps developed into towns, including Westcliffe. Reverend John Reininga designed the Hope Lutheran Church, located on the town's Main Street. Cast stone was used in the construction of the two-story building. The belfry, constructed above the front entrance, rose into a ninety-six-foot-tall gabled bell tower. Stained-glass windows graced all sides of the church. The interior featured a triple panel of stained glass depicting a biblical scene, as well as an ornately carved altar, created by Reverend Reininga. According to the prospectus obtained by the Office of Archaeology and Historic Preservation, the Hope Lutheran Church is believed to be the oldest Lutheran church in the state. (Colorado State Register, 5CR.55.)

In 1899, following the last great gold rush in Colorado, Teller County was created from portions of Park and El Paso Counties. The bustling mining town of Cripple Creek became the county seat. Today, Cripple Creek has been designated a National Historic Landmark District. A small clapboard structure served as the first house of worship for the Episcopalians in Cripple Creek. The horrific fires in April 1896 destroyed much of the town, including the church. The church bell was discovered in the rubble and stored for safe keeping. Under the leadership of Reverend Charles Y. Grimes, the new St. Andrew's Episcopal Church was built on the northwest corner of Carr Avenue and Fourth Street. The Queen Anne structure, built of brick, included arched windows and arches above the massing, culminating with three pedimented peaks over the church entrance. In 1957, the bell from the original structure was rediscovered, and a year later, it was installed in the current structure. It is local legend that the basement walls contain gold ore. (5TL.2.)

In 1892, St. Peter's Catholic Church was built on the hill at the northern end of Third Street. Bishop Nicholas Matz sent Father T. Volpe to serve as the first priest. Within a few short years, the parishioners had outgrown the church. In 1897, a new church of red brick was built on the site. With money donated by Cripple Creek's first millionaire, Winfield Scott Stratton, the Romanesque Revival structure featured a three-story bell tower crowned with a tall steeple. When completed, Father Volpe conducted the dedication ceremony. However, not long after the Easter High Mass in 1898, Father Volpe died. (5TL.2.)

The competing mining town of Victor claims the First Baptist Church among its entries in the National Historic Landmark registry. The founders of Victor, brothers Frank and Harry Woods, financed the construction of the church located at the northwest corner of Portland Avenue and Fourth Street. The Romanesque Revival church included a square three-story bell tower. For many years, the Woods brothers taught Sunday school at this church. (5TL.340.)

The area was originally known as Bayou Salado because of the rich salt deposits, but the region was renamed South Park by the miners. Now known as Park County, the area is a pristine valley surrounded by mountains.

Reverend Sheldon Jackson, a pioneer Presbyterian missionary, arrived in Denver in 1870. Jackson traveled the Presbyterian circuit where one of his first stops was the small mining community of Fairplay. There, Reverend Jackson formed and organized the first Presbyterian congregation in Park County. In 1874, Reverend Jackson built the South Park Community Church. Located at the southeast corner of Hathaway and Sixth Streets, the small church was built in the Carpenter Gothic style. The exterior, with its board-and-batten siding, included lancet windows and extensive wood trim. Lancet

Victor Baptist Church was built by the millionaire Woods brothers. *Author's collection.*

The South Park Church stands at South Park in Fairplay. *Courtesy of Jami Overholser Bevis.*

arches over the windows and doorway graced the Gothic structure. The steeply pitched roof supported an open bell tower capped with a hexagonal spire. Years later, the church was renamed the Sheldon Jackson Memorial Chapel. (National Register, 11/22/1977, 5PA.26.)

The town of Alma, at 10,355 feet, began as mining camp in 1873. In 1936, citizens of the community worked together to build the Alma Community Church. The simple rustic square building was constructed of native stone and included a pitched roof. The well-preserved building was placed in the National Register in December 1996. (5PA.438.)

In 1874, the Denver South Park and Pacific Railroad had reached the town of Morrison, an end-of-track railroad town. From there, passengers and freight were transferred to stage lines that continued the westward journey to the mountain mining towns. By 1878, the railroad had reached Bailey and pushed on to a third railroad depot thirteen miles west. David N. Cassell was agent for the Denver South Park and Pacific Railroad. Cassell was so taken with the beauty of the area that he filed for a homestead. As the railroad ran next to his property, Cassell erected a hotel and created a summer resort on his land. Cassell's resort was so popular that visitors proclaimed it "Cassell's

Garden." In 1894, Cassell built a lake, which was instrumental in the electric power plant he constructed in 1905.

In 1930, following Cassell's death, the property was purchased by Mary M. Dower. Under the auspices of the Mary M. Dower Benevolent Association, she created a religious summer camp, Camp Santa Maria, for boys and girls. In 1934, the Denver-based Northwestern Terra Cotta Company undertook the colossal project of erecting a statue of Christ high on the hill behind the camp facility. The statue, thirty-three feet high, was shaped in clay. Molding was then carefully placed around the large clay model. In order for the statue to fit into the ovens, it was carefully cut into 235 pieces. Terra cotta was pressed into each piece and then baked. The terra-cotta pieces were then transported to Camp Santa Maria. The tall base for the statue, twenty-two feet, was constructed of reinforced concrete and faced with terra cotta. A steel frame was attached to the base, and each terra-cotta piece was carefully attached to the steel frame. During this slow, tedious process, concrete was poured in several strategic places providing added strength and durability. For added safety measures, a lightning rod was installed, running down the back of the statue and into the mountainside. When completed, the statue was estimated to weigh some seventy tons. This statue of Jesus is the largest in the United States and second in size only to the *Cristo* in Rio de Janeiro.

In 1879, a portion of southwestern Lake County was formed into Chaffee County, named for U.S. Senator Jerome Chaffee. The mountain mining town of Granite served as county seat until the murders and intimidations during the Lake County War. Vigilantes terrorized the area, hanged people and threatened politicians, including county judge Elias Dyer, the son of Father John Dyer. Following the murder of Judge Elias Dyer, the county seat was eventually moved to Buena Vista in 1880 and then to Salida in 1928.

This statue of Jesus, above camp Santa Maria, is the largest in the United States and second in size only to the *Cristo* in Rio de Janeiro. *Courtesy of Denver Public Library.*

The following year, 1880, the St. Rose of Lima Catholic Church was built in Buena Vista. With help from the congregation, James Mahon and others hauled the lumber donated by fellow parishioner Thomas Starr's lumber mill, located in Poncha Springs. Constructed in the traditional Carpenter Gothic style, the steeped pitched roof was graced with an open bell tower. In 1969, the church building was moved to the edge of Colorado Highway 24 in an effort to save it from demolition. Now known as Park Chapel, the former church building serves as the Visitor Information Center for the Buena Vista Chamber of Commerce. (Colorado State Register, 3/10/1999, 5CF.176.)

The Grace Episcopal Church, located on the southwest corner of Park and Main Avenues, was built in 1883. Constructed in the Gothic Revival style, the wood-frame church included lancet window and door openings. The exterior was fashioned with board-and-batten walls, which resulted in a half-timbering appearance. The steep pitched, front gabled roof included a tall square open bell tower. Inside, the exposed timbered walls were trimmed with pendants and brackets accented by Gothic arches. When completed, the Grace Episcopal Church was consecrated, and the first service was given on Sunday, September 13, 1884. (National Register, 1/20/1978, 5CF.141.)

Gunnison County was named for John W. Gunnison, an early explorer who discovered what he thought was a great river but was actually a tributary of the Grand River, or Colorado River, as it was later named. Nevertheless, Gunnison named the tributary the Gunnison River. In 1876, the new town of Gunnison became the county seat.

The quaint small hamlet of Marble, located along the Yule River, is listed in the Colorado Historic Register. It was near the headwaters of the Crystal River that George Yule discovered an enormous outcropping of pure white marble in 1874. A few disgruntled gold miners in the area turned their attention to the fabulous native white rock. W.F. Mason, John Mobley, William Parry and William Woods each staked mining claims in the area. Soon, mining camps were established including Marble. In 1884, the first of five marble quarries opened in the Crystal River Valley. Knowing the popularity of marble across the country, John Cleveland Osgood, a principle stockholder in both the Colorado Midland Railroad Company and the White Breast Fuel Company, invested in stock options with several mining claims and marble quarries. In this keen business maneuver, Osgood provided the needed capital for the miners and quarry workers to process the enormous blocks of marble into smaller blocks suitable for shipping.[91] At the time, the only way to transport such large and heavy blocks of solid marble was by wagon to the Denver and Rio Grande depot at Carbondale. Over the years, the extraordinary Colorado marble would be used in the Colorado State Capitol building, as well as buildings across the country, including in Washington, D.C., where the largest block of Colorado Yule marble, fifty-six tons, was used to construct the Tomb of the Unknown Soldier.

Following the arrival of the railroad, the mining camp of Marble gradually became a town with fine houses, a school and a general store. Curiously, in those early years, a church was never built. In 1908, in what must have been an amazing transportation accomplishment, a church was actually brought to the town of Marble. The St. John's Episcopal Chapel, built in Aspen in 1886, was moved to Marble in 1908. The building was dismantled, loaded onto a flatbed rail car and shipped to Marble. Located at the corner of Second Street, the building was reassembled, and two rooms were added on each side, as well as a rear room. The additions served as a meeting room, a small library and a place for the local boys' club to gather. When completed, citizens of Marble renamed the church St. Paul's Church. The small clapboard church exhibited many features of the Gothic Revival style, including a steep pitched roof, topped with a marble cross. In 1911, a belfry was added, and a five-hundred-pound bell, cast by the New York firm of Moncy Bell Company, was installed. In 1985, the deed to the church was presented by the Episcopal Diocese to the congregation.[92] The historic church is listed in the Historic Resources of Marble, Colorado, as well as the National Register. (8/3/1989, 5GN.1355.)

Mesa County, so named for the large flat-topped mountain, was established in 1883. The town of Grand Junction was founded by George A. Crawford in 1881, following the government's forced removal of the Ute Indians. Situated near the confluence of the Grand River (renamed the Colorado River in 1921) and the Gunnison River, the infant settlement, as the county seat, soon became the hub for a branch of the Denver and Rio Grande Railroad. In 1882, George A. Crawford donated town lots to each of the local denominations. The following year, realizing that the black community of Grand Junction had been overlooked, Crawford deeded four lots to the "black citizens of Grand Junction" for one dollar each.[93] For the next nine years, members of the African Methodist Episcopal congregation worked to raise the money to build their church. By 1892, the members were able to pay cash for the building materials, $962.50, and began constructing their house of worship. William Austin not only hauled the brick to the building site, but he also laid the brick foundation. Elijah Hines, a Union veteran of the Civil War, was also one of the workers from the congregation instrumental

The St. John's Episcopal Chapel, built in Aspen in 1886, was moved to Marble in 1908. *Courtesy of Kenneth Jessen.*

in building the church. Although the structure was simple in architectural style, when completed, the congregation named its church Handy Chapel.

A few years after the opening of Handy Chapel, William Austin left Grand Junction for a better opportunity in Salt Lake City, Utah. In 1907, Austin's daughter, Lizzie Austin Taylor, an ordained minister and recently widowed, moved to Grand Junction to serve as minister of Handy Chapel. It was during Reverend Taylor's leadership that an addition to the church was constructed, again by members of the congregation.

In 1920, a small house was built adjoining the church. Known as Chapel House, it was used as a way station for travelers stranded in an era when there were few hotels for black people. Throughout the years, the members of Handy Chapel not only helped their own and those in the community, but Handy Chapel also became a beacon for the less fortunate: "We were always there to help the needy, so the Spirit helped us."[94]

So said Josephine Dicky, the great-granddaughter of William Austin, who helped build the church. Josephine was born in Grand Junction in 1924. She was twelve years old when her mother died. Just as the congregation of Handy Chapel had always helped those in need, the community came to the aid of Josephine's family: "When mother got so sick, there were white people who would come and stay with us. They would haul the water and heat it. They cooked and washed clothes for us. And they knew they were not going to get one penny. When my mother died, the white people of the town took up a collection and paid off all my father's debt. And, they got him a house."[95]

Reverend Lizzie Austin Taylor died in 1932. Her son, Booker Taylor, eventually served as minister at Handy Chapel. "Since they built this church, there's been a member of my family going here," said Josephine Dicky.[96]

At various times over the years when Handy Chapel was without a spiritual leader, traveling ministers were paid by the African Methodist Episcopal Church to officiate services and ceremonies. It was a practice that the congregation of Handy Chapel would come to regret. In 1980, the African Methodist Episcopal Conference filed a lawsuit claiming ownership of Handy Chapel. The lawsuit would drag on for eight years. During that time, Josephine Dicky, who served as caretaker of the church, was barred from the property. The new caretaker stripped the chapel bare. All fixtures and furnishings—including the chapel pews, pulpit and organ—were removed from the building. As the lawsuit dragged on, the building was rented out for a variety of purposes.

In the end, the court ruled that "the local black citizens" held the deed to the property, citing George A. Crawford's original 1882 deed to the "black citizens of Grand Junction" for one dollar each. Josephine Dicky and her daughter, Helen Dickey Wirth, regained ownership of Handy Chapel.

Years later, the historic chapel was placed on Colorado's Most Endangered Places List for 2011. Through generous donations, church members and community volunteers were able to repair the front porch entrance.

HistoriCorps, a preservation group modeled after the Civilian Conservation Corps and affiliated with Colorado Preservation Inc., spent a week working at Handy Chapel. During that time, the group replaced the roof, which had been covered with a tarp for more than a year. Patrick Eidman, manager of HistoriCorps, was impressed with Josephine Dicky, long since considered the heart and soul of Handy Chapel. In an interview with the *Denver Post*, May 7, 2011, Eidman said, "Josephine Dicky is a remarkable person. She gets here before the workers. She leads us in grace before lunch. She's a great inspiration for the crew. This is one of those projects that really grabs you by the heartstrings."

Perhaps it was due to Josephine Dicky's inspiration that Patrick Eidman and others with Colorado Preservation Inc. helped Dicky and the Handy Chapel congregation apply for grants from the Colorado State Historical Fund for restoration of the church and adjoining house. In August 2012, Handy Chapel received a $275,000 grant. Within a month, the firm of Chamberlin Architects began working on restoring Handy Chapel. There were many obstacles to overcome. The 1920 addition to the chapel had drastically deteriorated. It was determined that the underlying masonry was structurally unsound and close to collapsing. The Chamberlin Architects, along with Colorado Preservation Inc., agreed that the best approach was to "reconstruct the addition while preserving as much of the original materials as possible."[97] While this particular restoration process progressed, Josephine Dicky watched with great wonderment: "Josephine Dicky, passionate steward of Handy Chapel, finds great joy in running her hands over an exposed interior brick wall, brick that was laid by her great grandfather William Austin in 1892, brick that surrounds Josephine's grandson as he ministers to his flock during Sunday church service."[98]

With the historical restoration complete, there was one more obstacle: Handy Chapel was not in compliance with the Americans with Disabilities Act. Once again, the community came together, raising the additional $50,000 needed to build the necessary ramps and rails and a wheelchair lift for access to the church, as well as the compliance requirements to the restrooms. Overwhelmed by the community support, Josephine Dicky said, "I don't know why it takes loss and tragedy to bring out the good in people. It does to this day. I don't know what's the matter with us. That goodness is inside, but you don't always see it day to day."[99]

On Sunday, September 1, 2013, the dedication of the restored Handy Chapel took place in front of a packed audience. For the first time, the congregation saw the freshly painted church, both inside and out, as well

In Grand Junction, the African Methodist Episcopal congregation worked to raise the money to build its church in 1892. *Courtesy of Steve Robison.*

as new carpet, new bathrooms, ten new pews and a new altar, all within the original building that now included modern heating and air conditioning.

The dedication service was conducted by Josephine Dicky's grandson, John Paul, the fifth generation of Josephine's family to minister at Handy Chapel. (National Register, 8/19/1994, 5ME.4157.)

The western slope county of Delta was created in 1881, following the arrival of the Denver and Rio Grande Railroad. Lush green valleys and abundant rivers and creeks created an ideal area for farming and ranching. Delta, the county seat, was established that same year.

The First Methodist Church was built in 1891 at the northeast corner of Meeker and Fifth Streets. The simple clapboard building was replaced in 1910. Architect Samuel A. Bullard designed and built the new edifice in the English Tudor Revival style. Constructed of sand-colored brick from the Delta Brick and Tile Company, the two-story building included crenelated towers on each side. At the base of each tower, stairways were built to the double-doored entrance. These stairways were constructed of Wingate sandstone hauled from nearby Escalante Canyon. Neo-Tudor elements, such as parapets and wide arches, were incorporated in the doorways and several windows.[100]

Inside, the enormous sanctuary was graced with several windows of stained glass manufactured by the Midland Glass Company in Omaha, Nebraska. A large mezzanine or balcony surrounded a portion of the sanctuary with corner chancels. A unique feature of the sanctuary was the construction of the floor. Built on a low-grade slant from the back of the room, it allowed for better viewing. The ornately carved golden oak pews were purchased and shipped from the American Seating Company. (National Register, 2/20/1991, 5DT.896.)

Montrose County was created in 1882 following the arrival of the Denver and Rio Grande Railroad into the region. It was one of the state's richest agricultural areas, and the railroad added to the prosperity of the county. The Denver and Rio Grande depot gave rise to a new town also named Montrose.

In 1909, construction began for the Methodist Episcopal Church, located at the corner of First Street and South Park Avenue. Colorado Springs architect Thomas P. Barber designed and built the Romanesque Revival church. The large two-story edifice, built on a sandstone foundation, was constructed of yellow brick. Flanked on each side were matching tall square towers. The

The author at the door of the church in Lake City. *Author's collection.*

interior included several stained-glass windows, with many depicting biblical scenes. Several additions, changes and improvements were made over the years. In 1991, a significant change was made with the addition of a second wing of the church. The local architectural firm of Patrik Davis & Associates used matching yellow brick in the construction of the "educational" wing. Connected by a narrow stuccoed bridge, the new addition included a tower similar to the original flanked towers but was finished in rose-colored stucco. (Colorado State Register, 8/11/1999; National Register, 11/30/1999, 5MN.4493.)

Hinsdale County, one of Colorado's smallest counties, created in 1874, was named for local politician George A. Hinsdale. Within this county, some of the richest gold and silver discoveries were made. Mining camps were formed, and later towns were established, with Lake City being the most prominent. The former mountain mining town of Lake City is in the state and national historic registers.

A year after Enos Hotchkiss founded the town of Lake City, the Presbyterians were the first to build a house of worship in the new community. With the help of his parishioners, Reverend George Darley built the clapboard church, augmented with pedimented lintels. However, within a year, changes were quickly made. Because the door of the church was not wide enough to accommodate a casket for funeral services, a double-wide door was installed. The following year, 1879, Reverend Darley added a two-story manse next to the church, on the southwest corner of Fifth Street and Gunnison Avenue. Built in the Second Empire vernacular style, the L-shaped building included such features as bracketed lintels and double windows. The manse served as a living space for the reverend, as well as his successors.

In 1882, a sixty-foot-high bell tower was built above the entrance. The tower, built in the Second Empire vernacular style, featured two sets of lancet louvers on all four sides of the upper portion and just beneath the tall steeple. The bell for the tower was brought by wagon from Pueblo. That same year, the church acquired a reed organ.

Shortly after the bell tower was erected, Reverend Darley turned the leadership of the Presbyterian church over to his brother, Reverend Alexander Darley. Under the second Reverend Darley, membership grew, and the church became a vibrant part of the community. Today, the Presbyterian church in Lake City has the distinction of being the oldest still operating church on Colorado's western slope. (5HN.68.)

Two years after the Presbyterians built their church, the Catholics were ready to do the same. George Campbell, a local carpenter, submitted plans for a larger church, at a cost of more than $2,000. Campbell was selected by the church elders to build their church, but his plans were drastically scaled down. The small clapboard building included elements of Gothic architecture, such as the arched windows, while the bell tower featured a shingled steeple. When completed, the Catholic house of worship, just thirty-two by fifty-five feet, cost a little over $1,000 to erect. St. Rose of Lima Catholic Church, so named for the first canonized saint of the Americas, was completed in 1877. The St. Rose of Lima Catholic Church served the Lake City community for more than one hundred years. Then, in 1980, what began as a renovation process nearly resulted in the demolition of the historic church. During the process, it was discovered that structural weakness was the result of a deteriorating foundation. The congregation worked together to raise the necessary funds needed for repairs. Eventually, $50,000 was raised, which paid for the new foundation, new floor, new roof and an updated heating system. Today, St. Rose of Lima Catholic Church continues to serve the citizens of Lake City. (5HN.68.)

In 1891, the First Baptist Church was built at the west end of Lake City's Bluff Street. The clapboard edifice included elements of Carpenter Gothic and Queen Anne architecture. A forty-five-foot steeple towered over the church entrance. Inside, Tiffany stained-glass windows imported from France graced the sanctuary. Curiously, folding opera chairs were used rather than pews. (5HN.68.)

Ouray County, formed in 1877, was named for Ouray, the Ute chief who worked his entire life keeping the peace between two cultures. The county seat was the mountain mining town of Ouray. Ouray's Episcopal congregation are credited with establishing the town's first church on the southwest corner of Fourth Street and Fifth Avenue. Built with Cornish miners' extraordinary masonry skills, the church exhibits elements of English Tudor designs. The interior of St. John's Episcopal Church included intricate wainscoting by local carpenters. A unique feature was the wooden altar screen. In 1876, a parish hall was built next to the church. More than one hundred years later, in 1988, St. John's Episcopal Church received a much-needed renovation, including a new roof and stained-glass windows. Inside, another stained-glass window featured a scene that the artist Virginia Laycock called "God's Gift to Ouray." (5OR.585.)

On the opposite corner from the St. John's Episcopal Church, the First Presbyterian Church was erected on the northwest corner of Fourth Street. Reverend George M. Darley, who in 1875 had built the Presbyterian Church in Lake City, did the same for the Presbyterians in Ouray.

During its construction in 1890, Reverend George Darley was forced to adhere to the approved plans from the Presbyterian Erection Board in Philadelphia, Pennsylvania. Thus, the church, erected in the Queen Anne style, was void of Reverend Darley's personal touches. Over the years, the church sustained fire damage and went through a series of renovations. During one of the renovations, a new red metal roof was installed, as well as the installation of Palladian windows.

In 1938, after the town's first school was demolished, a belfry was erected on the church grounds to house the original school bell. (5OR.585.)

Created in 1883, San Miguel County was named for the San Miguel River, which flows from its headwaters high in the San Juan Mountains. When gold was discovered in the San Juan region, the mining town of Telluride emerged in 1878. Following the creation of San Miguel County, Telluride became the county seat.

One of Telluride's first churches was St. Patrick's Catholic Church. Located on the northwest corner of Galena Avenue and Spruce Street, the Gothic Revival architectural style also included elements of the classic Carpenter Gothic style, such as clapboard siding and Gothic arched windows. Above the entrance, which featured a round stained-glass window, the steeply pitched roof supported an elongated gabled bell tower. Inside, the Tyrol hand-carved Stations of the Cross were simply stunning. Father Cornelius O'Rourke, who helped build the church, also served as the first leader of the congregation. (National Register, 5SM.321.)

San Juan County was one of the many additional counties following Colorado statehood in 1876. The rich silver mines, high in the San Juan Mountain region, brought an economic boost not only to the southwest portion but also to the entire state. With such economic growth, mining camps developed into towns. The town of Silverton became the county seat in 1876. Three years later, citizens learned that the Denver and Rio Grande Railroad had begun laying tracks toward Silverton. The *La Plata Miner* extolled the opportunities to come in an editorial printed in the December 29, 1879 issue: "Silverton, 'queen of the silver land,' is about to begin a boom for this country that will not cease growing for a hundred years to come. In fact, it is impossible to estimate the great advantage in every way the completion of this road will be to our camp."

One of those "advantages" the newspaper editor wrote of came about just a year after the arrival of the railroad. Reverend Joseph Pickett had arrived in Silverton in June 1879. After meeting with the local Congregationalists in the area, Reverend Pickett was able to arrange for Sunday services to be held in the schoolhouse. For the next year, the Congregationalists of Silverton held fundraisers to build their own church. In August 1880, the group acquired the corner lot on Reese and Eleventh Streets. Reverend Pickett conducted the cornerstone-laying ceremony, his last religious act in Silverton before moving on to other mining towns to continue on his Congregational mission.

With help from church members, Pastor Harlan Roberts began construction of the United Church of Silverton. Built in the Carpenter Gothic style of architecture, a steep pitched roof stabilized a single chimney. Gothic arched windows graced the sides of the church, and an arched doorway greeted the worshipers. At the corner of the building, the base of a steeple was erected, which rose just above the A-frame entrance to the church. Four years later, a parsonage was built next to the church. Constructed in the same Gothic style, elements of Neoclassical architecture were evident, such as the polished wooden trim used around the windows and doors. Finally, in 1886, the steeple of the church was completed, topped with an iron weathervane. Today, the United Church of Silverton has the distinction of being the oldest Congregational church on Colorado's western slope. (Colorado State Register, 5SN.59.)

In 1883, Bishop Joseph Machebeuf arrived in Silverton via the new Denver and Rio Grande Railroad to organize the building of St. Patrick's Catholic Church. In 1884, the local Catholic congregation built a small frame church on Tenth Street. However, by 1905, the building could no longer hold the growing membership. The building was sold to the African Methodist congregation. Under the direction of Father Cornelius O'Rourke, who had recently arrived from Telluride, a new location for St. Patrick's Catholic Church was selected at the corner of Tenth and Reese Streets. Father O'Rourke and the Catholic congregation enlisted Denver architect Frederick W. Paroth to design and build the new St. Patrick's Catholic Church. Before the foundation was laid, tragedy struck the congregation. Father O'Rourke and close friend John McComb took a leisurely horseback ride along the Las Animas River. Suddenly, Father O'Rourke's horse bolted, throwing the priest off the horse and into the rushing waters of the Las Animas River. John McComb jumped into the river in an effort to save his friend. Both bodies were later recovered from the river.[101]

After a respectful mourning period, construction of the church commenced. The Romanesque Revival church was built of natural stone, with much of the masonry work done by local miners. The many windows were framed with rounded trim, as was the double door. The bell tower, erected above the church entrance, was a square open structure, supported with four corner minarets and topped with a Celtic cross. The following year, 1906, the rectory was built adjacent to the church. (National Register, 5SN.59.)

In 1958, the Catholic Men's Club of the St. Patrick's Catholic Church, with the leadership of Father Joseph Halloran, erected a shrine to honor the church and their savior, Jesus Christ. The Catholic Men's Club selected a site at the base of Anvil Mountain, with the approval of San Juan County officials. Local stonemasons built a base for the marble statue, with a surrounding low wall. Behind the stone base, a grotto, also of stone, was erected. Many of Silverton's citizens donated money to purchase the Carrara marble statue of Christ. Depicted with outreaching arms, the five-ton statue stood twelve feet high. When completed a year later, a road was built, Scenic Drive, which joined the end of Tenth Street, leading to the Christ of the Mountains Shrine.[102]

La Plata County, formed in 1874, was named for the La Plata Mountains. In 1880, Durango, the railroad town of the San Juans, became the county seat. General William Jackson Palmer, the founder of the Denver and Rio Grande Railroad, envisioned a prosperous town that would thrive after the arrival of his train. To achieve that end, Palmer sent his partner, Dr. William Bell, to the area to lay out the town of Durango. Palmer and Bell created the Durango Trust, by which free lots would be donated to organizations to build churches, schools and parks. The first to receive a free lot were the Methodists in 1881, who built a church on the southwest corner of Third Avenue and Eleventh Street. The Carpenter Gothic architectural elements included arched windows and a steep pitched roof. The corner entrance, with two separate arched doors, allowed for worshipers to enter from either street. Above the entrance a tall square belfry rose, towering above the pitched roof. Just one week after the Durango Methodist Church was completed, the first service was held on Sunday, January 15, 1882. The following day, the *Durango Herald* printed an editorial extolling the new church: "The new church is the finest yet completed in our Infant city." After fire destroyed portions of the church in 1889, repairs were made and a parsonage was added. (Colorado State Register, 5LP.304.)

The Presbyterians built their house of worship on the southeast corner of Third Avenue and Twelfth Street. Unfortunately, in 1889, fire destroyed the church. In 1890, the cornerstone for the new First Presbyterian Church was laid at the same location. The Brooklyn, New York architectural firm of L.H. Volk and Sons was hired to design and build the church. Constructed of native stone, the Queen Anne edifice featured a shake-shingle roof. Several stained-glass windows were graced with rounded wood trimming. The open bell tower, with large arched windows, was crowned with a shake-shingle steeple. In 1903, a large manse was constructed next door. (Colorado State Register, 5LP.304.)

Despite the repeal of the Sherman Silver Purchase Act in 1893, Colorado's mining industry managed to retain much of its holdings throughout the state. In fact, new ore strikes in the form of gold at Cripple Creek and silver high in the mountains of the western slope saved the state from economic disaster. So rich were the silver discoveries that legislation was quickly passed to create Mineral County in 1893. The storied mining camp of Creede became the county seat.

Two years earlier, in 1891, a wandering prospector by the name of Nicholas C. Creede picked through a rock outcropping along Willow Creek, a few miles above its junction with the mighty Rio Grande. Realizing that the streak embedded in the rock was indeed silver, he hollered to his partner a cry of "Holy Moses!" Creede filed his claim, aptly named the Holy Moses Mine. Creede's find yielded an average of nearly $5,000 per ton. A mining camp was quickly established, named Creede in his honor. By the following spring, a building frenzy had occurred, a town committee had been formed and the mining camp had slowly developed into a town.

During the first year of Creede's existence, Sunday church services were typically held in one of the many saloons in the mining camp. The *Creede Candle* reported on one of the first Sunday services in the February 18, 1892 issue: "Last Sunday was long on religious services. Rev. Joseph Gaston of Ouray preached in the Creede hotel that morning to a large congregation, and in the evening occupied the desk of the keno roller in the club room of Watrous, Bannigan & Co.'s saloon."

It was during this time that Reverend E.A. Paddock began raising funds for his Congregational church and was assisted by the town's gambling kingpin, Jefferson Randolph "Soapy" Smith. Henry Edwards, a friend of Smith's, later spoke of Smith's involvement in the establishment of the first church in Creede:

At the time Creede, Colo., was booming, Smith went there. He was instrumental in founding the first church there. The minister came to "Soapy" and asked his assistance in soliciting funds. The two collected $68, to the minister's dismay, but "Soapy" came to the rescue. "Give the money to me," said "Soapy," "and I will show it to some of my friends and shame them into giving more. I will be back in a little while." In an hour, Smith returned and put $600 into the hands of the happy parson. He [Smith] had gone to a gambling house and won $600 with the $68. The parson did not learn until years afterward where "Soapy" had "gathered" the money with which they built their church.[103]

Reverend E.A. Paddock, grateful for Smith's financial assistance, acquired a lot at the corner of Creede Avenue and Fourth Street. With Smith's money, Paddock hired men to construct his church. The *Rocky Mountain News* reported on the progress of the church and Smith's involvement in the March 7, 1892 issue: "Just below his [Smith's] place one's ears are this Sabbath night fairly split with strains of music from the various dance halls on the other side of the street. Directly across from the unfinished building in which are neither doors or windows or plastering on this cold Sabbath night, float the sweet strains of music."

When completed, Reverend Paddock's Congregational Church was the first house of worship in Creede. In 1905, Reverend Paddock's Congregational Church was torn down and rebuilt. The enormous replacement, built in the Queen Anne style, was built of red brick. Local sandstone was used in framing the many stained-glass windows, as well as the arched doors. The steep pitched roof supported a corner belfry tower. (5ML.)

In 1897, the Immaculate Conception Catholic Church was built at the corner of Main and Third Streets. Constructed in the traditional Carpenter Gothic style of architecture, the Catholic church served the Creede community for nearly eighty years. In 1974, the small white-frame Catholic church was moved to the edge of the town's Sunnyside Cemetery, located a half mile west of the town. (5ML.)

At the height of Colorado's mining boom, the richest ore was coming from the San Juan Mountains in the southwestern portion of the state. Legislation was passed to create Rio Grande County in 1874. The mining supply towns of Del Norte and Monte Vista vied for the title of county seat, which Del Norte eventually claimed.

The Methodist church located at the northwest corner of Seventh and Pine Streets was built in 1876. The natural sandstone building offered a double entry from either street. Gothic arched windows were placed on either side of the entrance. The dedication service drew crowds from all over the county, as the keynote speaker was none other than suffragette Susan B. Anthony. (Colorado State Register, 5RN.1585.)

In 1881, the Catholic Archdiocese approved the Roman Catholic parish of St. Francis of Assisi Catholic Church in Del Norte. The Hispanic adobe edifice was topped with a pyramidal roof, which supported a bell tower. Shortly after completion of the church, a cemetery was established next to the church. As the years went by several additions to the church were made, a new shingle roof replaced the original and the adobe walls were painted white. (Colorado State Register, 5RN.532.)

In 1898, a second Catholic church was built. Holy Name of Mary Catholic Church was built on the opposite corner where the Methodist church stood, at Pine and Sixth Streets. Holy Name of Mary Catholic Church was constructed of local rhyolite. Several Gothic arched windows, all set with stained glass, graced the exterior as well as the interior. Inside, a spectacular hand-carved altar was flanked with life-

Leadville's many churches are included in this collage. Annunciation Catholic Church (*center*) was the scene of Margaret "Molly" Brown's wedding, as well as the funeral for Elizabeth "Baby Doe" Bonduel McCourt Tabor. Today, the tall white steeple can still be seen from miles around. *Courtesy of Denver Public Library.*

size religious figures. Years later, a chapel was added, as was a rectory. (Colorado State Register, 5RN.581.)

Although the mining supply town of Monte Vista lost the claim as the seat of Rio Grande County, the arrival of the Denver and Rio Grande Railroad brought prosperity to the town. According to local historian Patricia Sanchez, "The Presbyterians came into Conejos and Rio Grande counties in the 1880s, establishing churches in Antonito, Alamosa, Del Norte, Mogote, San Rafael, and Monte Vista. They also established schools in the area and had a large number of Hispanic converts."

The first of the Presbyterian churches in the region was built in Monte Vista in 1888. The small frame church was replaced in 1899. Located on the corner of Broadway and Second Avenue, the construction of the First Presbyterian Church was indeed a group effort. Several church members volunteered their time, labor and individual skills and talents. James Campbell, a stonemason, used coarse gray-colored rhyolite blocks quarried at Myers Stone Quarry for the exterior of the church. The unique cross-gabled roof included an open bell tower. The interior also received the same local attention to craftsmanship and detail as the exterior. Charles Ydren, a Swedish immigrant, carved much of the woodwork, including the doors, pews and altar.

In 1956, the First Presbyterian Church celebrated its seventy-fifth anniversary. In a remembrance journal, titled "People of the Book," a parishioner, Bernice Martin, recalled the following: "The organ required a small boy sitting behind a screen to pump it, and sometimes the boy became inattentive and forgot to pump at critical moments, or actually went to sleep. The pay was 25 cents per Sunday. Many men still in the congregation remember their youthful experiences as boy pumper of that organ." The First Presbyterian Church is listed in the Colorado State Register. (5RN.512.)

Several years after the establishment of the Monte Vista Cemetery, efforts were made in 1898 to improve and "beautify" the burial ground. In 1912, Denver architect George Harvey was commissioned to build a chapel at the cemetery. Constructed in the Craftsman architectural style, the cemetery chapel is the only such structure representative of this type of architecture in Rio Grande County.[104] (Colorado State Register, 8/11/1999, 5RN.646.)

In 1922, the First Methodist Episcopal Church was built at 215 Washington Street, constructed of "purple tapestry" brick and enhanced with a "salt glaze." The brick firing and glazing method was abandoned when America entered World War II in 1941. No other building constructed of this unique style exists in Rio Grande County or the entire San Luis Valley. (Colorado State Register, 6/11/2003; National Register, 10/11/2003, 5RN.782.)

Notes

Chapter 1

1. Howlett, *Life of Bishop Machebeuf*.
2. Walters and Young, *More Prairie Tales*, 30.
3. Noel, *Buildings of Colorado*, 270.
4. Archives of the Zion Baptist Church, Denver, Colorado.
5. Noel, *Denver Landmarks & Historic Districts*, 183.
6. *Denver Post*, October 24, 1998.
7. Smith, *Horace Tabor*, 314.
8. Ibid., 315.
9. Wommack, *From the Grave*. Following the death of Elizabeth "Baby Doe" Tabor, Horace's remains were disinterred and reburied next to his wife at Mount Olivet Cemetery.
10. Noel, *Denver Landmarks & Historic Districts*, 185.
11. Noel, *Colorado Catholicism*, 343.
12. *Denver Post*, October 24, 1998.
13. Directory of Religious Properties, Colorado Historical Society, 2010.
14. Brettell, *Historic Denver*, 115.
15. Records of the Colorado State Register of Historic Properties, held at the Colorado History Center.
16. Ibid.
17. Brettell, *Historic Denver*, 64.
18. Ibid., 69.

19. Records of the Colorado State Register of Historic Properties, held at the Colorado History Center.
20. Noel, *Colorado Catholicism*, 357.
21. Ibid., 64.
22. Ibid.
23. Archives of the Colorado Archdiocese, Denver. Also see Noel, *Colorado Catholicism*, 70.
24. Archdiocese of Denver.
25. Archdiocese of Colorado, "History of Our Lady of Mount Carmel."
26. Noel, *Colorado Catholicism*, 36.
27. Wommack, *Murder in the Mile City*.
28. Shikes, *Rocky Mountain Medicine*, 163.
29. Ibid.
30. Ibid.
31. Noel, *Colorado Catholicism*, 12.
32. Ibid., 73.
33. Ibid.
34. Ibid., 328.
35. Beaton, *Colorado Women*, 204.
36. McQuarie, *Littleton Colorado*, 59.

Chapter 2

37. Scott, *Slade!*, 64.
38. Wommack, *From the Grave*.
39. St. Vrain Valley Historical Association, *They Came to Stay*, 196.
40. Ibid.
41. Wommack, *From the Grave*.
42. Office of Archaeology and Historic Preservation, Colorado State Register, 5JF.420.
43. Messinger and Rust, *Faith in High Places*, 56.
44. Smith, *History of St. James Church*, 7.
45. Ibid.
46. Ibid., 8.
47. Ibid., 15.
48. Ibid., 22.
49. Granruth, *Guide to Downtown Central City*, 21.
50. Noel, *Buildings of Colorado*, 204.

51. The mountain communities of Idaho Springs, Georgetown and Silver Plume are all in the Colorado State List of Historic Properties and thus have the same county registration number.

52. Morton, *Dyer, Dynamite & Dredges*, 4.

53. Ibid., 10.

54. Ibid., 14.

55. Noel, *Buildings of Colorado*, 462.

56. Three of the officers buildings moved to the new town now serve as the White River Museum. Among the many artifacts on display are the wooden plow Meeker used that ignited the fury of the Utes, as well as his printing press used to print the *Meeker Herald*. Colorow's peace pipe is also among the Ute collection.

57. Messinger and Rust, *Faith in High Places*, 65.

58. Ibid.

59. Bancroft, *Famous Aspen*, 23.

60. Tread of Pioneers Museum Archives.

61. *Steamboat Pilot*, December 9, 1927.

62. The author and her second godson were both baptized in this church on the same day, during a ceremony in April 1985.

63. Museum of Northwest Colorado, *Early Craig*, 54.

Chapter 3

64. Lavender, *Bent's Fort*, 154. The re-created Bent's Fort is in today's Otero County.

65. Ibid., 11.

66. Wommack, *From the Grave*.

67. Carson letter was dated April 16, 1868. Simmons, *Carson & His Three Wives*, 175.

68. Shikes, *Rocky Mountain Medicine*, 236.

69. Sides, *Blood and Thunder*, 395.

70. The bodies of Carson and his wife, Josefa, would later be reburied in the cemetery at Taos, New Mexico.

71. Messinger and Rust, *Faith in High Places*, 102.

72. Norman, *In and Around Old Colorado City*, 51.

73. Wommack, *Colorado's Historic Mansions and Castles*.

74. Messinger and Rust, *Faith in High Places*, 79.

75. Directory of Religious Properties, April 2010.

76. Wommack, *From the Grave.*
77. Letter on file at the Colorado Historical Society.
78. Von Bamford, *Leadville Architecture,* 68.
79. Blair, *Leadville,* 123.
80. Ibid.
81. Von Bamford, *Leadville Architecture,* 29.
82. Messinger and Rust, *Faith in High Places,* 46.

Chapter 4

83. The ruins of the original chapel can still be seen.
84. Wommack, *From the Grave.*
85. Noel, *Buildings of Colorado,* 412.
86. Lopez-Tushar, *People of El Valle,* 56.
87. Noel, *Colorado Catholicism,* 12.
88. Lopez-Tushar, *People of El Valle,* 56.
89. Feitz, *Alamosa!,* 15.
90. Gunnison Avenue in Saguache later became a portion of U.S. Highway 285.
91. Nelson, *Marble & Redstone,* 20.
92. Messinger and Rust, *Faith in High Places,* 72.
93. Handy Chapel Archives, Grand Junction, Colorado.
94. *Grand Junction Sentinel,* September 1, 2013.
95. *Denver Post,* May 7, 2011.
96. Ibid.
97. Handy Chapel Archives, Grand Junction, Colorado.
98. Ibid.
99. *Denver Post,* May 7, 2011.
100. Noel, *Buildings of Colorado,* 532.
101. Messinger and Rust, *Faith in High Places,* 50.
102. Smith, *Brief History of Silverton,* 98.
103. *Denver Post,* November 15, 1914. Also see Smith, *Alias Soapy Smith,* 232.
104. Wommack, *From the Grave.*

Bibliography

Primary Sources

Colorado State Register of Historic Properties.
El Paso County Court Records, Colorado Springs, Colorado.
History of Clear Creek, Boulder and Gilpin Counties. N.p.: O.L. Baskin & Company, 1880. Reproduced in 1971.

Archives and Additional Sources

Archdiocese of Colorado.
Archdiocese of Denver.
Colorado History Center. Reverend T.A. Rankin's detailed diary, housed at the history center.
Colorado Preservation Inc.
Denver Public Library Western History Department. Memorial booklet for Father Leo Heinrichs.
Directory of Religious Properties, Colorado Historical Society, 2010.
First Church of Divine Science Archives, Denver, Colorado.
Handy Chapel archives, Grand Junction, Colorado.
History of Our Lady of Mount Carmel.
Tread of Pioneers Museum Archives, Steamboat Springs, Colorado.
Zion Baptist Church Archives, Denver, Colorado.

Books

Bancroft, Caroline. *Famous Aspen*. Boulder, CO: Johnson Publishing Company, 1955.

Beaton, Gail M. *Colorado Women: A History*. Boulder: University of Colorado Press, 2012.

Blair, Edward. *Leadville: Colorado's Magic City*. Boulder, CO: Pruett Publishing, 1980.

Brettell, Richard R. *Historic Denver*. Historic Denver Inc., 1979.

Feitz, Leland. *Alamosa!* Little London Press, 1976.

———. *Cripple Creek!* Little London Press, 1967.

Granruth, Alan. *A Guide to Downtown Central City, Colorado*. Self-published, 1989.

Howlett, William J. *Life of Bishop Machebeuf*. Originally published in 1898, reprinted by Regis College, 1987.

Lavender, David. *Bent's Fort*. Lincoln: University of Nebraska Press, 1954.

Leyendecker, Liston E. *The Griffith Family & the Founding of Georgetown*. Boulder: University of Colorado Press, 2001.

Lopez-Tushar, Olibama. *The People of El Valle, Pueblo, CO*. N.p.: El Escritorio Publishing Company, 1997.

McQuarie, Robert J. *Littleton Colorado*. Friends of Littleton Library, 1990.

Messinger, Jean Goodwin, and Mary Jane Massey Rust. *Faith in High Places*. Roberts Rinehart Publishers, 1995.

Morton, Jane. *Dyer, Dynamite & Dredges*. The Father Dyer United Methodist Church, 1990.

Museum of Northwest Colorado. *Early Craig*. Charleston, SC: Arcadia Publishing, 2013.

Nelson, Jim. *Marble & Redstone: A Quick History*. Blue Chicken Publishing, 2000.

Noel, Thomas J. *Buildings of Colorado*. Oxford University Press, 1997.

———. *Colorado Catholicism*. Boulder: University Press of Colorado, 1989.

———. *Denver Landmarks & Historic Districts*. Boulder: University Press of Colorado, 1996.

Norman, Cathleen. *In and Around Old Colorado City: A Walking Tour*. Preservation Publishing, 2001.

Pulcipher, Robert S., Lyle W. Dorsett and Eugene H. Adams. *The Pioneer Western Bank: First of Denver, 1860–1980*. Denver, CO: First Interstate Bank of Denver, 1984.

Royem, Robert T. *America's Railroad*. Durango & Silverton Narrow Gauge Railroad Museum, 2007.

Scott, Bob. *Slade!: The True Story of the Notorious Badman*. Glendo, WY: High Plains Press, 2004.

Shikes, Robert H., MD. *Rocky Mountain Medicine*. Johnson Books, 1986.

Sides, Hampton. *Blood and Thunder*. New York: Doubleday, 2006.

Simmons, Marc. *Carson & His Three Wives*. Albuquerque: University of New Mexico Press, 2003.

Smith, Duane A. *A Brief History of Silverton*. Western Reflections Publishing, 2004.

———. *The History of St. James Church*. St. James Church, n.d.

———. *Horace Tabor: His Life and the Legend*. Boulder, CO: Pruett Publishing, 1973.

Smith, Jeff. *Alias Soapy Smith*. Juneau, AK: Klondike Research, 2009.

St. Vrain Valley Historical Association. *They Came to Stay*. Longmont, CO, 1971.

Von Bamford, Lawrence. *Leadville Architecture*. N.p.: Architecture Research Press, 1996.

Walters, Hildred, and Lorraine Young. *More Prairie Tales*. Self-published, 1976.

Williams, Lester L. *Cripple Creek Conflagrations: The Great Fires of 1896 that Burned Cripple Creek, Colorado*. Monument, CO: Filter Press, 1994.

Wommack, Linda. *Colorado's Historic Mansions and Castles*. Charleston, SC: The History Press, 2014.

———. *From the Grave: A Roadside Guide to Colorado's Pioneer Cemeteries*. Caldwell, ID: Caxton Press, 1998.

———. *Murder in the Mile City*. Caldwell, ID: Caxton Press, 2016.

Index

About the Author

A Colorado native, Linda Wommack is a Colorado historian and historical consultant. She has written ten books on Colorado history, including *Ann Bassett, Colorado's Cattle Queen*; *Cripple Creek Tailings*; *Murder in the Mile High City*; *Colorado's Landmark Hotels*; *From the Grave: Colorado's Pioneer Cemeteries*; *Colorado Gambling: The Early Years*; *Our Ladies of the Tenderloin: Colorado's Legends in Lace*; *Colorado History for Kids*; *Colorado's Historic Mansions and Castles*; and *Haunted History of Cripple Creek and Teller County*. She has also contributed to two anthologies concerning western Americana.

Linda has been a contributing editor for *True West Magazine* since 1995. She has also been a staff writer, contributing a monthly article for *Wild West Magazine*, since 2004. She has written for the *Tombstone Epitaph*, the nation's oldest continuously published newspaper, since 1993. Linda also writes

for several publications throughout her state.

Linda's research has been used in several documentary accounts for the national Wild West History Association and historical treatises of the Sand Creek Massacre, as well as critical historic aspects for the new Lawman & Outlaw Museum in Cripple Creek, Colorado, which opened in 2007.

Linda feeds her passion for history with activities in many local, state and national preservation projects and participating in historical venues, including speaking engagements, hosting tours and involvement in historical reenactments across the state.

As a longtime member of the national Western Writers of America, she has served as a judge for the acclaimed national Spur Awards in Western Americana literature for eight years. She is a member of both the state and national Cemetery Preservation Associations, the Gilpin County Historical Society, the national Wild West History Association and an honorary lifetime member of the Pikes Peak Heritage Society. As a member of Women Writing the West (WWW), Linda has organized quarterly meetings for the Colorado members of WWW for the past ten years and served on the 2014 WWW Convention Steering Committee. Linda currently is serving her third term as a board member and is the chair for the DOWNING Journalism Award.